THE E-LEARNING
REVOLUTION

The Chartered Institute of Personnel and Development is the leading publisher of books and reports for personnel and training professionals, students, and all those concerned with the effective management and development of people at work. For details of all our titles, please contact the Publishing Department:

tel. 020-8263 3387

fax 020-8263 3850

e-mail publish@cipd.co.uk

The catalogue of all CIPD titles can be viewed on the CIPD website:

www.cipd.co.uk/publications

THE E-LEARNING REVOLUTION

From propositions to reality

Martyn Sloman

Chartered Institute of Personnel and Development

Typeset by Fakenham Photosetting Limited, Fakenham
Printed in Great Britain by the Short Run Press, Exeter

British Library Cataloguing-in-Publication Data
A catalogue record for this book is available from the British Library

ISBN 0-85292-873-4

Chartered Institute of Personnel and Development
CIPD House, Camp Road, London SW19 4UX
Tel: 020-8971 9000   Fax: 020-8263 3333
E-mail: cipd@cipd.co.uk Website: www.cipd.co.uk
Incorporated by Royal Charter. Registered Charity No. 1079797.

CONTENTS

List of Case Studies		vii
Acknowledgements		viii
Preface		ix
Introduction and Propositions		xi
1	**The Connected Economy**	1
2	**What Is Happening in Training?**	24
3	**A New Paradigm for Training**	53
4	**Developing the Agenda for the Organisation**	75
5	**Focusing on the Learner**	108
6	**The Changing Role of the Trainer**	138
7	**Training in Transition**	159
8	**Trainers and the New Economy**	179
	Index	197

DEDICATION

For all those who hold schoolteacher values, especially those who have taught at Hywel Dda School, Ely, Cardiff.

LIST OF CASE STUDIES

Chapter 1   BBC Online
Chapter 2   Cap Gemini Ernst & Young Virtual Business School
Chapter 3   Performance feedback at Ernst & Young
Chapter 4   CERN
              Hanover Housing Association
              Clifford Chance
              The Post Office
              IBM's Global E-Learning Model
Chapter 5   Learning at Motorola University – EMEA
              British Airways Quest and Communication points
Chapter 7   MDA training
              Dove Nest Group
Chapter 8   learndirect

ACKNOWLEDGEMENTS

I would like to begin my acknowledgements by expressing my gratitude to the following colleagues at Ernst & Young: Mike Laws, Julie Holden, Toby Hoskins and John Odell. Special thanks also go to my immediate boss, Des Woods. Our conversations yielded almost daily insights and ideas from Des that have found their way into the text.

The following people assisted by reading drafts: Karen Jaques, Iain Thomson, Steve Knight, Richard Comber, Mike Staunton and Sara Willis. Mark Van Buren and Pat Galagan of the American Society for Training and Development and Elliott Masie of the Masie Centre generously found time to share thoughts and ideas. I am grateful to the many other people who allowed me to draw on their work and have acknowledged this at appropriate points in the text.

Lorna Munro undertook some of the work on the case study organisations. I am grateful to her and to all the representatives from the companies cited who shared their experiences and perceptions so openly. Kim Andrews typed and organised the manuscript and showed immense patience in meeting tight deadlines. Nicola Gray and Jo Kesbey also helped me with the production of case studies and figures. Thanks also to the staff of the CIPD Library – especially Steve Corbett – and to Anne Cordwent, my editor, for her encouragement and support.

Most of this text was written in Norfolk where my wife Anne has tolerated sustained weekend and holiday work on the book. She has been totally understanding and sympathetic. My thanks to her for her support in all my life's efforts.

PREFACE

This book is written from the point of view of a practising human resource manager. I have been fortunate to have worked in the profession that I enjoy, and consider to be thoroughly worthwhile, for the past 20 years. For the last decade, I have served as the head of a training function in a number of organisations. There have been numerous changes over the 20-year period – most of them beneficial in that they have enabled human resources and corporate training to become more effective. New approaches to business strategy, with more emphasis on competition through people, is one example. The emergence and acceptance of competencies and the growing use of competency frameworks is another.

Nothing, however, approaches the gains to be won from the connected economy. This term, and its underlying elements, will be explored and explained more fully in the chapters that follow. In essence, however, the interlinking of computers and the acceptance of communication protocols through the World Wide Web have created the Internet. This will force us to do our jobs in a totally different way.

I was very pleased to be asked by the Chartered Institute of Personnel and Development (CIPD) to write a book on these challenges and opportunities. It was both an exhilarating and a daunting request. Exhilarating in that it allowed me the opportunity to make a public contribution to an important debate, which will have profound implications on the future of my chosen profession. Moreover, our cumulative decisions on the adoption of new Internet-based training could have important social consequences. They could influence who will, and who will not, have access to opportunities for self-development in the new economy.

It is a daunting request, however, because the subject is moving so rapidly that any material requires permanent updating and addition. It is never the right time to publish. Each section calls for a health warning that the information was correct at November 2000 when the manuscript was completed.

Two factors have encouraged me to proceed and face the near certainty that a proportion of my suggestions or predictions will be
overtaken by events – or simply proved to be wrong.

First, there is an evident need for a book that offers practical assistance for all those managers who are contemplating the transition to
a new delivery of training in their organisation. Their jobs will
differ: they could be human resource professionals (especially training managers), working in information technology or knowledge
management or have more general line responsibilities. Whatever
their titles and responsibilities, a book exploring the issues is
required now. It should be written by someone who is himself or her-
self grappling with the problems.

Second, I am fortunate that Ernst & Young has fully supported my
endeavours. They have given me permission to publish and allowed
me to include material from the workplace. Many of my ideas have
been drawn from or developed as a result of discussions with my colleagues in the firm.

Martyn Sloman

INTRODUCTION AND PROPOSITIONS

Two related developments are combining to demand a new approach to the effective delivery of training in organisations. Both are a consequence of the information-rich or connected economy. The first is a step-change in the capability and potential of technology-based training. The second is a shifting business model: the way that organisations compete and society advances.

Together these developments will transform the way that everyone in human resources will do their jobs and the skills they require. In particular they will call into question the role of training and its place in the organisation. They will redefine the distinction between training and learning. They will eliminate the barriers between training, knowledge management and performance management. They will shift responsibilities between the manager, trainer and individual. They will, in time, blur the boundaries between internal and external providers of training and redefine the market for both training products and delivery. They will demand a reorientation of the learning support required.

There is a huge opportunity here. The rules of the game have been changed and everyone concerned with effective training must adapt. So far, the agenda has been driven by those who created the technical opportunities. It is now essential that those who will manage their application and implementation understand what is happening and develop appropriate responses. The alternative is a failure of credibility for the profession and a lot of costly and embarrassing mistakes in the organisation.

This book is intended to help those involved in decisions on the provision of training to acquire a clear understanding of the underlying issues. Once this has been achieved, a realistic agenda can be created. Every organisation faces different challenges, but some basic messages apply throughout.

> **Focus Point 1: Central questions for those involved in training**
>
> What do we need to know about the connected economy (and how do we find out)?
>
> What do we need to do (what is the most effective organisational response)?
>
> How will the connected economy affect me in my organisation (how will it alter my role and responsibility for training)?
>
> How will it affect our world (what is the wider economic and social impact on training)?

The relevant questions posed by the emergence of the connected economy are set out in Focus Point 1.

The answers to these questions are wide-ranging, so this book is part primer and part polemic. It is partly an introduction to the issues and partly a controversial writing or argument. Hopefully together these two components will provide a framework that will lead to effective decision-making and allocation of resources. To assist application, practical examples will be offered where possible. To signpost the book's scope and arguments in advance, a series of 21 propositions are set out below. These propositions summarise the main conclusions that have been reached as a result of the research and analysis undertaken to produce this book. They provide a framework to guide the actions of those involved in directing, managing or supporting the training function, irrespective of the role or title. The propositions will summarise an argument or offer general advice. Taken together they offer a useful summary of the contents.

21 propositions

1   The Internet changes everything, including training (see pages 1–7).

2   The drivers of Internet activity and development are business and commercial: they will shape and foreshadow developments in training (see pages 7–13).

3   The connected economy gives rise to a blurring of activities and of boundaries (see pages 13–19).

4   There is a danger of becoming seduced by the functionality of the technology, rather than concentrating on its use (see pages 42–44).

5   Training will move from events to interventions (see pages 44–47).

6   The distinction between learning and training is of value and should be maintained (see pages 54–63).

7   There will be a convergence (or blurring) between knowledge management, performance management and training. All are responses to gaining competitive advantage through people in the information age (see pages 64–69).

8   E-learning can give new meaning to the concept of the learning organisation (see pages 69–70).

9   A new paradigm based on learner-centred interventions will emerge. This will draw on business, learning and traditional training models (see pages 70–71).

10   Training managers should identify the appropriate wins in their organisation rather than letting the availability of technology determine their agenda (see pages 77–82).

11   Training professionals should investigate the new business models. They should review their value chains (see pages 82–85).

12   E-learning will be most effective for the acquisition of knowledge and least effective where interpersonal interaction is needed for learning (see pages 85–86).

13   E-learning will be most effective as part of a systematic approach involving classroom and experiential learning with appropriate support (see page 86).

14   A new discipline of learner support will emerge and should be encouraged (see pages 108–120).

15   There will be renewed interest in learner motivation, learning styles and time and space to learn (see pages 120–127).

16   Three distinct functional specialisms for trainers will evolve: design, delivery and learner support (see pages 139–142).

17   A useful distinction can be made between hard technology and soft technology. The expertise of many trainers is in soft technology and this offers them an attractive future (see pages 142–156).

18   Any part of the training supply chain that does not add value will disappear. Other parts could well become commodity products (see pages 161–164).

19   Time, not spend, will become a scarce resource. Monitoring of use and evaluation of effectiveness will become critically important (see pages 164–171).

20   Social inclusion is emerging as a key political issue. Trainers have the power to influence the debate positively (see pages 179–187).

21   More honesty and less hype is required if the training profession is to grasp the new opportunity to maximum effect (see pages 188–192).

Chapter 1

The connected economy

Foresight is always better afterwards[1]

Introduction

The statement that 'the Internet changes everything' is attributed to Larry Ellison, the founder and head of the software giant Oracle. In a speech delivered in Geneva in 1996, he predicted that the day of the personal computer was over and that the Internet was the vehicle of the future. Many of his competitors treated this prognosis with derision. Oracle prospered.

Twenty-one propositions will be introduced in the course of this book: the first is set out immediately below:

Proposition 1

The Internet changes everything, including training.

Of course the statement as it stands should not be taken as a literal truth. Some things, which lie outside the economic and commercial arena, may not be altered. The point is that the Internet is bringing about a change that will affect all economic relationships. It will alter the context in which we all operate.

What, then, are the likely effects of the Internet on training? The question is of critical importance. The pursuit of an answer must begin with an understanding and definition of terms, in the area of both technology and training. It will continue by looking at the effect that the Internet has had on the market economy.

The connected economy and the Internet

The emergence of the Internet has been considered as significant and far-reaching a change as the invention of the internal combustion engine and its application in motorised transport. The information age, it is claimed, could herald as dramatic a transformation as the machine age, which introduced electricity to homes and mechanisation to industry.

At the heart of what is happening now is the connectivity of computers and the establishment of a network with protocols – a set of rules that governs the transmission of data. Enhanced computer power has assisted all forms of activity for almost half a century. Gordon Moore, founder of Intel Corporation, is credited with the articulation of Moore's Law: simply, this states that every 18 months computer processing power doubles while cost holds constant. The connected economy is something beyond more powerful data processing and offers huge opportunities in all facets of shared activity.

As is widely recognised, the important breakthrough came in the early 1990s. Tim Berners-Lee – working at CERN (the European Laboratory for particle physics) and building on earlier developments in information technology – proposed an approach and standards that would allow access to data from any source. In this way the World Wide Web was 'invented'. A full account of the impressive early years is contained in Tim Berners-Lee's book *Weaving the Web*.[2] From the mid-1990s, use of the Internet has spread to the point where it has become universally recognised as the dominant commercial and social force at the turn of the twenty-first century. Focus Point 2 gives an indication of the magnitude of its impact.

‹It is about much more than the arrival of a new platform for the delivery of training›

Today's training professionals are therefore operating at the beginning of a revolution. Importantly it is about much more than the arrival of a new platform for the delivery of training. The context in which the trainer operates, internal and external relationships and

> **Focus Point 2: The impact of the Internet**
>
> The US Department of Commerce[3] has compiled information on the time that it has taken for a critical invention or breakthrough to reach 50 million users. The comparative figures are:
>
> - radio   38 years
> - PC   16 years
> - television   13 years
> - Internet   4 years
>
> The speed of penetration and commercial impact of the Internet to date has been both dramatic in volume and consistently under-estimated. The US company Forrester, which specialises in research for the Internet, produces annual estimates of Internet trade. The April 2000 forecasts[4] were labelled: Global eCommerce Approaches Hypergrowth. This suggested that world Internet trade would rise from $657.0 in 2000 to $6,789.8 billion in 2004. By that time it will represent 13.3 per cent of total US sales and 8.6 per cent of world sales.

the role itself can be expected to undergo profound changes. The rapid developments in computer power have given the trainer the potential of new information technology tools to assist delivery over the desktop using personal computers. This impact of enhanced technology is one phenomenon; connectivity and the Internet are something else again. To understand the opportunities created by this upheaval it is helpful to start with an agreed terminology. Some key definitions are set out in Focus Points 3 and 4.

Different writers and different organisations use different terms. A number of these will be encountered as their ideas and approaches are considered. In general, throughout this book, e-learning will be adopted as the preferred term. It will be used as a shorthand for e-learning/e-training as defined in Focus Point 4 – the delivery of learning and training that takes advantage of connectivity. Where necessary or appropriate, the term technology-based training will be used to describe applications that specifically do not take advantage of connectivity. These could for example include the use of CD-ROMs accessed through a stand-alone computer that is not net-worked or connected to other uses.

Focus Point 3: Key definitions on connectivity[5]

Connected economy – an economy in which networked computers affect the market for goods and services.

Connectivity – the process by which computers are networked and can share information.

Extranet – a collaborative network that uses Internet technology to link organisations with their suppliers, customers or other organisations that share common goals or information.

Internet – the global computer network of digital information linked by telecommunication systems and using common address procedures and protocols.

Intranet – a company-based version of the Internet. Large organisations have set up their own intranets as an aid to internal communications and may include training material or other information as part of them.

World Wide Web (often abbreviated to Web or www) – the network of documents accessed through the Internet using the protocols. In a sense it is the publishing side of the Internet, giving access to text, graphics and multimedia information that has been placed on 'sites' or 'pages'.

One of the more important implications of operating in a connected economy is that arguments over the most effective or appropriate platform for training that uses technology are over. Training will be delivered though the Internet/intranet using web protocols. It will be accessed through personal computers and laptops and feasibly using mobile technology.

‘The arrival of the Internet is a disruptive technology for the training profession’

Focus Point 4: E-training and e-learning[6]

Training – the process of acquiring the knowledge and skills related to work requirements using formal, structured or guided means, but excluding general supervision, job-specific innovations and learning by experience.

Learning – the physical and mental process involved in changing one's normal behavioural patterns and habits.

> **‹ Learning lies within the domain of the individual; training lies within the domain of the organisation ›**

The value of differentiating between learning and training will be discussed later in the book. As a first outline, however, the simple distinction should be noted. Learning lies within the domain of the individual, can result from a whole range of experiences, and can be positive, negative or neutral from the organisation's point of view. Training lies within the domain of the organisation: it is an intervention designed to produce behaviours from individuals that have positive organisational results.

On this basis ...

E-learning/e-training – the delivery of learning or training using electronically-based approaches – mainly through the Internet, intranet, extranet or Web (the 'e' is a shortening of 'electronic', originally popularised for e-mail, the transmission of messages digitally through a communication network). The terms m-learning/m-training are emerging, with the 'm' denoting 'mobile' for wireless technology using mobile telephones.

Clayton Christensen of Harvard Business School, writing in 1997[7] introduced the term 'disruptive technology'. This is a technology that overturns a traditional business model and makes it much harder for the established firm, with its own cultural inertia, to embrace. Those who have invested time, money and effort in the previous business model resist. The biggest impact of a disruptive technology may come when it gives rise to entirely new products.

The arrival of the Internet is a disruptive technology for the training profession. Clayton Christensen's analysis should be heeded. Existing models will be overturned; many trainers will resist. The losers in the profession will be those who through cultural inertia remain inside their own comfort zone and think in terms of traditional models. A starting point should be to look outside and see what can be learned from an analysis of the impact of the Internet on business and economic activity.

New rules for competition

Disruptive technology offers great opportunities as well as threats. However, to echo Clayton Christensen's argument, if the training profession is to capitalise on these opportunities, it must look outside its own sphere of activity. It must seek to understand the way in which the rules of economic activity are transformed.

As a starting point, it should be recognised that the Internet:

- provides a new information system
- introduces a new marketplace
- offers a new system of communication
- establishes new methods of distribution.

Significantly, the above apply across all sectors of the economy. Historically, the emergence of railways had their initial impact on the transportation of goods – although there was an unexpected subsequent effect on the leisure industry. The Internet has been pervasive from the start. It is global: it provides a worldwide method of sharing up-to-date information instantaneously. It is cheap: it would be difficult to cite an innovation where the costs of access were so small – this helps to explain the rapid spread of the Internet.

Much of the economic analysis and discussion has concentrated on what can be called the market effect: the way in which the Internet brings about greater competition through facilitating the exchange of goods and services. The market effect is summarised in Focus Point 5.

Two practical illustrations of the market effect are set out in Focus Point 6. Both have evident implications for human resource activity. The first illustration, on fund management, offers an excellent example of the way that the forces of change alter training require-

Focus Point 5: The market effect

The Internet alters the nature of competition: it alters the rules of the game. This outcome is achieved through:

- gains for the consumer through increased awareness
- transparency of information – especially price information.

This means that more markets have and will become commodity markets, where competition is based on price alone, rather than on the superior knowledge that suppliers can offer the customer.

A market moves to a commodity market when the superior knowledge of suppliers becomes open to all. A good example is the travel industry. Anyone who wishes to book a low-cost holiday or a cheap flight can proceed by surfing the Internet and supplying credit card information on the Internet or by phone. As a result the expertise of the specialist travel agent is devalued. Information is there for all to see and all can take advantage. Competition on price becomes more important and the structure of the industry will change.

Transparency of information makes whole processes more efficient. It drives down prices and/or brings enhanced value to the customer by delivering other benefits. The new technology in general and the Internet in particular has unquestionably been a major engine in the high growth/low inflation enjoyed in the UK and other Western countries at the beginning of the twenty-first century.

ments through the need for new or enhanced skills in the organisation. The second illustration – of the ways in which these forces will affect recruitment – describes a situation which is evolving and on which the current impact of the Internet is less certain. Together these examples helpfully introduce the second proposition.

Proposition 2

The drivers of Internet activity and development are business and commercial: they will shape and foreshadow developments in training.

Focus Point 6: Illustrating the market effect

Fund management

The 2000 report *Fund Management: New skills for a new age*[8] argued that UK investment houses must redesign their executive development programmes to cope with the online economy.

One of the powerful drivers for change follows from Internet technology: passive, patient customers are turning into active, demanding clients. Other drivers follow from liberalisation, deregulation and an overhaul of the rules for conducting business. Generally, globalisation and the arrival of e-business will dramatically accelerate the rate of change.

One fund manager working for an international outfit was quoted in the report as saying:

> The golden days of high margins are over. Moreover, we are getting more mandates for smaller sums of money as pension funds use the information available through the Internet to check out investment performance and spread their portfolios.

Professor Rajan argued that UK firms will only benefit if they alter their approach and develop new skill sets. 'Business as usual is no longer an option.' Product differentiation and customer management skills will grow in importance.

Online recruitment

In February 2000, Forrester, the research organisation specialising in the Internet, produced a report on online recruitment.[9]

The report suggested that both recruiters and consumers agreed that online recruiting is more efficient than newspapers or hiring agencies. Moreover, online job-seeking grew with Internet experience: 'Experienced users were twice as likely to have searched for a job online than a new user.'

However, the Internet was still far less influential than personal referrals or newspapers and the uneven quality of jobs, unproductive résumé tools, and over-delivery of résumés are holding back progress (résumé is the US term for CV).

Most significantly, recruiters:

plan to increase online spending 52 per cent by 2004, primarily at the expense of print advertising and search agency fees.

Given the inefficiencies in the current market and the possibilities created by the Internet, Forrester predicted the emergence of a new breed of site – 'a career network'. This would develop a longer-lasting, more valuable relationship with users and companies. Forrester defined the career network in the following terms.

one-stop career management site that aggregates multiple career services for consumers and recruiters and serves both in an ongoing relationship.

Three components will reside at the heart of the career network:

- A *profile database:* by offering a range of services in career-related and non-career-related areas, these large sites will grow a profile database consisting of 1) explicit user data – résumés, salary levels and news preferences, and 2) implicit data – interests and hobbies gleaned from online behaviour.
- A *jobs database:* aggregating jobs from numerous sources, this database stores detailed data on companies, job demand and the types of positions filled online.
- A *matching engine:* this database engine not only matches candidates to jobs, but also learns preferences. Users who reject job matches are not shown similar jobs. Recruiters who reject candidates are not shown similar candidates.

The market effect is one way in which the Internet will affect training in organisations. Effective training is needed if an organisation is to compete (in the private sector) or achieve its objectives (in the public/voluntary sector) through the enhanced capability of its people. The skills required of those people will be altered by the new competitive environment. Moreover, the training market is a market like any other. The way in which this service will be supplied, and the roles and relative power of the agents or participants in the training market, will undergo a dramatic shift.

The implication behind Proposition 2 is that, by examining the way the Internet has affected business and commercial interactions, some important pointers can be gained for training. Again, to emphasise a recurrent theme throughout this book, those responsible can no longer focus on their own narrow environment. They must look outside.

For the remainder of this chapter some analyses of the business effects of connectivity and the Internet will be presented. Each offers different insights and, where published works are cited, the reader is recommended to seek out the original – and, above all, reflect on the applicability of these insights for his or her situation. These are not asides!

The Economist survey

On 26 February 2000 *The Economist* magazine produced a special supplement on e-commerce.[10] The starting point of *The Economist*'s analysis is that the main impact of the Internet to date has been on business-to-business (B2B): transactions that take place between companies rather than between companies and consumers. According to Forrester Research, in 1999 80 per cent of e-commerce transactions were business-to-business. The main focus of *The Economist*'s survey was on retailing. Although the absolute level of consumer e-commerce was small, it is much higher in some sectors – retail, stockbroking and books, for example.

In all markets the Internet has the ability to generate different price and exchange mechanisms. It allows product and price comparisons to be made using up-to-date information generated anywhere. It encourages auctions and other forms of exchanges to take place. It can bring together (and create communities amongst) buyers and sellers throughout the world.

The influence of the Internet extends beyond the trade itself. It is used as a place to seek information. Critically, the Internet allows continuous updating and real-time information.

An inevitable effect of all this must be an intensification of competition. This will produce benefits to consumers in the form of lower prices and more choice at the expense of producers and intermediaries (for example, wholesalers). This will lead to large-scale restructuring of industries. The rules of the game are changed.

'The Internet does not replicate the social function of shopping'

Access to information on a global basis offers a huge advantage to the customer. Updating of demand is continuous so firms can compete without investing in large physical sites or carrying stocks in warehouses. The offer to customers need not be a physical offer. However, the Internet does not replicate the social function of shopping (the casual interchange with an assistant or fellow shoppers). Nor does it produce the change in atmosphere that some people enjoy in a shopping centre. *The Economist* survey therefore distinguishes between 'high touch' and 'low touch' goods and services. The former are goods and services that the consumers prefer to see and touch before purchase (shoes are a good example); the latter are those where individuals do not need such reassurance (books and CDs). To date, low touch items sell best on the Internet. For similar reasons, the Internet may work well for replacement buys rather than new purchases. Fulfilment (the completion of the order and its delivery to the customer) will always be an issue.

Looking forward, technological change will improve speed and capacity – and availability of access. It is not a matter of snappier websites. The exciting opportunities will arise from the proliferation of broadband (or high bandwidth) Internet connections to the home. (Bandwidth is the capacity of a data connection or network for digital transmission – it is analogous to the number of lanes on a road.)

Another feature of e-commerce is that the Internet generates data, which can then be exploited. To quote from *The Economist*:

> Everything can be recorded: not just every transaction, but which webpages a customer visits, how long he spends there and what banner he clicks on. This can produce a formidable array of data that makes possible both one-to-one marketing – directing sales pitches at particular individuals – and 'mass customisation' – changing product specifications, for instance in jeans or computers, to match individual orders to individual customer preferences.[10]

The Internet will also have a significant effect on the value or supply chain. This can be defined as: 'a system whose constituent parts include material suppliers, production facilities, distribution services and customers linked together via the forward flow of materials and the forward and backward flow of information.' One argument, certainly in retailing, is that it is possible to eliminate many of the links in the chain altogether. Manufacturers can sell directly to consumers. Dell Computers is a good example: it has developed a successful business directly, first by telephone and subsequently via the Internet. The phrase 'disintermediation' (meaning the elimination of unnecessary intermediaries through direct transactions) has been used to describe changing markets for financial investment products for more than two decades. It is now applied to e-commerce. However, what may be happening is a subtler change: the Internet is changing the role and function of intermediaries, not necessarily eliminating them. This is a concept of considerable importance to the training market and will be discussed later in that context.

The Economist survey has a specific focus on retailing. The important thing is for those involved in training to seek insights, use analogies and recognise opportunities from the changing business model. For example, if learners are regarded as consumers, how can the data that they produce when using web-based training be used to customise and thus improve the product for them? To take a second example, how will changes in the role of intermediaries (including their possible elimination) reshape the training industry? These, and similar issues, will be discussed in later chapters of this book.

Blur

The term 'connected economy' formed part of the subsidiary title of an influential book by two US authors, Stan Davis and Christopher Meyer. The former is a senior fellow and the latter director of the Cap Gemini Ernst & Young Center for Business Innovation in Boston. *Blur: The speed of change in the connected economy* was published in 1998.[11]

Davis and Meyer argued that the economy (the way people use resources to fulfil their needs) is undergoing a fundamental shift driven by three forces:

Speed   Every aspect of business and the connected organis-
               ation operates and changes in real time.

Connectivity   Everything is becoming electronically connected to

everything else: products, people, companies, countries, everything.

Intangibles   Every offer has both a tangible and intangible economic value. The intangible is growing faster.[11]

Speed concerns the shortening of product life cycles and the
use of electronic networks to transfer messages and information.
Connectivity is about the use of computing power, not for data processing but for connecting people to people, machine to machine,
product to service, network to network, organisation to organisation,
and all combinations thereof. Intangibles is a more difficult concept to
grasp. Davis and Meyer argue that the intangible portion of the economy has grown and that this growth has altered how we see the world.
Services have come to dominate the economy. Information is more
available and will continue to increase in importance: all products now
have a service component; emotions, the trust and loyalty that people
feel for a brand, are significant influences on economic activity.

Together speed, connectivity and intangibles coalesce and interact to
create what the authors call the blur economy. A business (or other
activity) is never at rest or in focus – everything is blurred. There is a
blur of desires, where product and services meld into one to become an
offer and buyers and sellers merge. There is a blur of fulfilment, where
strategies and organisations merge. There is a blur of resources, where
people can no longer separate their working and consuming selves.

One of the continuing themes of this book is that those involved in
training urgently need to consider the implications operating in a
blur economy. The word blur will appear frequently in later sections
of the text – with thanks to Stan Davis and Chris Meyer.

Blur is a powerful and seductive insight. Its importance to this book
is summarised in the third proposition.

Proposition 3

The connected economy gives rise to a blurring of activities and
of boundaries.

The concept of blur is apparent when some of the more popular web-sites are examined. In some cases the underlying business model (the way that they will generate income and profits) is far from evident. At this stage in the development of the Internet it may be that with the ready availability of venture capital support, some organisations are simply testing the market to see what develops.

Sometimes, however, a site proves so popular that it almost achieves a life of its own. It can grow and develop in response to the demand of users, while still maintaining its original purpose and objective. Such a site is BBC Online. This forms the first of a series of case studies that will be included at the end of the chapters in this book.

One of the current pieces of accepted wisdom in e-learning is the need to market sites. A common quotation is 'If you build it, he will come.' This is thought most definitely *not* to be the case in e-learning. (The words, from W. P. Kinsella's novel *Shoeless Joe*, were spoken by a baseball announcer to an Iowa farmer who wished to build a baseball diamond for the legendary long-dead baseballer Shoeless Joe Smith.)

In fact, as the BBC Online case study illustrates, sometimes if you build it people *will* come.

E-transformation

This chapter has considered the changes brought about through connectivity – and how they affect commercial and economic activity. Connectivity is a key driver of globalisation. Other forces that will affect organisations are growing consumer awareness and liberalisation/deregulation – the relaxation of the rules that restrict trading. All of these forces reinforce each other and lead to a changing business model.

Connectivity is especially powerful. Boundaries separating different organisations and activities have become increasingly irrelevant (or blurred). Connectivity focuses on the exploitation of current and emerging technologies to transform business connections with customers, suppliers, partners and internal stakeholders. The first of these is currently served by the Internet/extranet; the last (internal stakeholders) by the intranet. Next-generation technology will, of course, create new channels and blur these opportunities.

‘'e' is much bigger than just trading electronically’

It should now be recognised that 'e' is much bigger than just trading electronically using the Internet. It is changing the way that organisations communicate and undertake transactions. Entirely new companies based on new business models are emerging. Focus Point 7 below is drawn from an internal Ernst & Young document and summarises the components of these new models.

Ernst & Young has developed a series of tools to enable organisations to build an e-business model (e-business rather than e-commerce is Ernst & Young's preferred term). One of these tools, the Transformation Framework, can helpfully be introduced at this stage. It is reproduced as Figure 1. Such tools are known as single frames: a diagram on one page that captures key concepts in graphical form. A number of single frames will be presented in the course of this book.

The Transformation Framework is used to determine the extent to which clients wish to transform their organisation towards an e-

Focus Point 7: Key components of new business models

- Low-cost access to global markets/suppliers.
- Reduced marketing and sales costs for businesses.
- Twenty-four-hour shopping and reduced costs for customers.
- Elimination of traditional intermediaries and emerging new intermediaries.
- Further/cheaper connections between businesses, leading to reduced costs and increased agility in the supply chain.
- Enhanced communication with internal stakeholders leading to faster responses and improved speed to market.
- New entrants into markets supplying completely new offerings, potentially eliminating existing players in that market.

[Reproduced by permission of Ernst & Young]

Figure 1

ERNST & YOUNG TRANSFORMATION FRAMEWORK

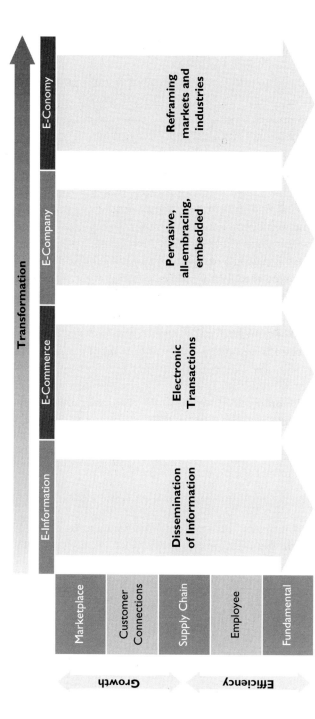

business and to identify specific initiatives to support this goal. Importantly, it shows four states of this transformation.

Stage I: E-information – dissemination of information

At this stage, the organisation will have an online presence (necessarily seven days a week, 24 hours a day) that will provide one-way information over the Internet. Dissemination of information to whatever source (customer, suppliers, employees) is faster, cheaper and more reliable.

Stage II: E-commerce – electronic transactions

Here the web output is fully integrated with the existing processes and systems that serve the traditional channels. Data usage improves: data entry is required only once and knowledge can be disseminated and leveraged throughout the organisation. Data-sharing with suppliers is made possible.

Stage III: E-company – pervasive, all-embracing, embedded

In this third stage, as much as possible, all functions of the business are conducted in a networked environment. E-business is the normal method for transaction amongst trading partners. Customers are dealt with online and the data is used to create greater loyalty. There is much greater efficiency in the supply or value chain. There is greater awareness gained through higher-quality information. This allows senior management to assess business profitability more rapidly and to manage processes more effectively.

Stage IV: E-conomy – reframing markets and industries

This is the most fully realised state of e-business. Change extends beyond the boundary of the organisation. A new economic system has emerged in which business is conducted electronically and each economic element is adapted to support e-business. An aggregated solution, or one-stop shop, has emerged. Everything from products, services, to internal knowledge systems and learning is accessed through compatible electronic gateways. New efficiencies are secured as a matter of course.

The Transformation Framework is of particular assistance in emphasising the stages of transition. It is a concept that can be applied across all goods and services. The left-hand column (marketplace, customer connections, supply chain, employee, fundamentals) indicates the all-embracing nature of the change. The framework will be reintroduced in Chapter 4, where it will be used to assist in developing an agenda for the training professional in his or her organisation.

The impact on training

It is now appropriate to move from a general consideration of the connected economy and its business impact to focus on training. The next two chapters will look at the changes in the training environment: first by undertaking a brief overview of current developments, and second by reviewing the prevailing conceptual models and their relevance in the new connected economy.

It is hoped that the discussion so far has appeared neither irrelevant nor depressing. Of the two, dismissal as irrelevant would be more disturbing. The changes driven by connectivity are profound and – to return to the opening sentence of this chapter – the Internet changes everything. Much of the analysis, insights and arguments that have been introduced in the wider economic context in this chapter will reappear in different forms and at different stages throughout the book. An attempt will then be made to relate them specifically to training issues and later to the role of trainers. The hope is that the discussion so far will have already led the reader to translate the general observations on connectivity to his or her specific challenges.

The speed of change is frightening, but should not lead to depression. Some readers may recall that, in the Old Testament book of Daniel, writing appeared on the wall at King Belshazzar's feast. Part of the message indicated that the days of the Kingdom were numbered; part of the message indicated that the King had been weighed in the balance and found wanting. There is writing on the wall for the training professional (and, indeed, in this blurred connected economy there are all sorts of messages everywhere). It does not, however, present such a dire message. Instead it demands that our practices and approaches are changed if we are to add value to the modern economy and our own organisation. The start of that process is to understand some implications of the changes that are taking place – that has been the objective of this chapter.

‘Take comfort from the fact that our situation is not as acute as that of King Belshazzar’

A certain amount of uncertainty and anxiety is inevitable and desirable – no one knows where the changes are leading us. Time, however, is of the essence and fellow training professionals can take comfort from the fact that our situation is not as acute as that of King Belshazzar who, according to the Old Testament, was slain that same night.

References

1   The aphorisms at the beginning of each chapter are all attributed to one individual: the US baseball hero, Lawrence 'Yogi' Berra, who played 18 seasons for the New York Yankees between 1946 and 1963 and subsequently managed both New York teams. He was renowned for the pithy but seemingly confused sound bite. The samples reproduced here are all taken from the following website on 'The Jurisprudence of Yogi Berra': www.law.emory.edu/ELJ/volumes/spg97/yogi.html.

2   BERNERS-LEE T. *with* FISCHETTI M. *Weaving the Web.* London, Orion Business Books, 1999.

3   US Department of Commerce 1998, *The Emerging Digital Economy*, www.ecommerce.gov/emerging.htm.

4   Forrester Forecasts, *Global eCommerce Approaches Hypergrowth.* Forrester Research, April 2000.

5   Most of the definitions have been adapted by the author, but the following text is recommended: *The IPD Guide on Training Technology.* London, Institute of Personnel and Development, 1998. The following Internet sites are recommended for definitions of more specialist technological terms: www.webopedia. com *or* www.whatis.com.

6   SLOMAN M. *A Handbook for Training Strategy.* Second edn. Aldershot, Gower, 1999. pp.xviii–xix.

7   CHRISTENSEN C. *The Innovator's Dilemma*. Boston, Harvard Business School Press, 1997.

8   RAJAN A. *Fund Management: New skills for a new age*. Sussex, Centre for Research in Employment and Technology in Europe (CREATE), 2000. www.create-research.co.uk.

9   LI C. *The Careers Network*. Cambridge, Mass. Forrester Research, 2000.

10   'Shopping around the Web: a survey of e-commerce'. London, *Economist Publications*, supplement to 26 February 2000 edition. www.economist.com.

11   DAVIS S. *and* MEYER C. *Blur*. Oxford, Ernst & Young/Center for Business Innovation/Capstone, 1998. (www.blursite.com)

Case Study

BBC ONLINE

Introduction

The British Broadcasting Corporation was one of the first organisations to appreciate the potential of the Internet. The BBC is a public-service broadcaster, and education and learning feature, and will continue to feature, heavily in its content and activity. Given its success, there has been some controversy about the commercial implications of the initiative. Some competitors have expressed anxiety, and some politicians opposition, arguing that this is not a proper activity for the BBC. Partly as a response, the BBC maintains two major sites: www.beeb.com, which is managed by BBC Worldwide, emphasises its global reach, contains advertising and merchandising and is unashamedly commercial; and www.bbc.co.uk, which is operated as a public service. www.bbc.co.uk/education was a pioneering initiative in e-learning and is the subject of this case study.

The development of the site

The site originated through the activities of programme makers, particularly Jonathan Drori, now head of commissioning, BBC Online, and George Auckland, now head of digital media at BBC Education. In the late 1980s internal discussion between them and others led to a recognition of the potential of the Internet. It should be remembered that there were no browsers available at the time so the initial interest was in textual fact sheets.

In the mid-1990s momentum developed as websites were associated with TV and radio programmes: particularly prominent here were the TV series *This Multi-Media Business* and *The Net*, and the radio series *The Big Byte*, all of which considered the rise of information technology. It was recognised that websites could extend beyond fact sheets, and funding was secured to explore ways of interacting with the audience.

The BBC Networking Club was established in 1994 by BBC Education. This was primarily an intervention to help people access and use the emerging Internet. The Networking Club acted as an early Internet service provider.

The BBC website grew as more programmes required a supporting website, and there was a risk of incoherent content. To cope with the growth, considerable thought was given to effective navigation tools, and the site has received plaudits. In 2000, BBC Education Online won the Judges Award from the Royal TV Society for its educational impact. This is one of the highest accolades in the industry.

Current learning content
One of the significant successes of the site is its continuing link with the public examination system. It offers education support for the learning process – often linked with broadcast programmes.

GCSE Bite Size was introduced in 1996. This supports the demands of the school examinations with cross-media activity: publications, a television series and a website. The popularity of this site has grown exponentially. Server capacity has needed updating to cope with the hits. Demand is very seasonal, but at its height the site received some 2.5 million visits a week.

More generally for adults there is extensive educational content material on a range of subjects, including science, history and health. Some of it is linked to programmes; if so, efforts are made to ensure that the material has a shelf-life beyond the programme's. Some of the content is generic and not so closely aligned with broadcast activity.

A series of approaches has been developed to encourage learning action with the public. BBC Alert (www.bbc.co.uk/alert) provides customised information about the whole of the BBC: factual broadcast output, web links and related local events. Users can either use the website to view webpages that match their selections or register for a weekly e-mail version to match their preferences. Elsewhere on the BBC site, users can create their own version of the BBC Home Page using the 'my BBC' facility. There are also many BBC message boards and moderated discussion groups, some of which are clearly recreational (the *Eastenders* site is the most popular), but others have an important educational content (the teen site provides a good example).

Perhaps the most important feature is the sheer volume of use of the BBC site as a whole (www.bbc.co.uk) covering news, education and general interest; it has the highest access of any content site in Europe.

Future development
The early development of the site reflects an idealism and a vision about the values and importance of public-service broadcasting. Broadcast TV and radio can stimulate interest in a variety of educational activities – they form one end of a chain. At the other end is the consumer/user/listener: he or she has the power to undertake activity and create or produce results. In between are intermediaries who can engage, guide and communicate. The BBC initiative started as a content provider: some of the challenge must lie in influencing the intermediary parts of the chain. Inevitably, being the high-profile public organisation that it is, its activities will be subjected to scrutiny.

Amongst future intentions is one to make available a full set of materials for the national curriculum in digital form. This will demand a rigorous and complete coverage of all content.

For adults, the emphasis will be on the concept of a learning journey. This will offer an appropriate environment for interaction in individual educational exploration. George Auckland emphasises the importance of 'bite-size, on demand and just in time'. In his view a learning module of whatever form should be available in slots of about 12 minutes' duration. The environment for adults should be as seamless as possible. Technology should assist, not intrude.

Jonathan Drori sees other challenges ahead. The technological methods of access will include desktop devices like PCs, domestic TV and radio and mobile devices. As broadband develops, so they will all be able to access consistent if not identical information. This will assist learning opportunities but present an organisational challenge for the BBC. The digital divide – the division between those who have the skills and equipment to get ready access to Internet and those who do not – could widen. Other challenges will follow from the global reach of the BBC's Online service: 35 per cent of its traffic comes from outside the UK and its online news service has a high reputation. It would be optimistic to think that the BBC can continue to be a pioneer; it does, however, remain an examplar of a web-based intervention.

My thanks to Jonathan Drori and George Auckland for their assistance in the preparation of this case study.

Chapter 2

What is happening in training?

You observe a lot by watching

The previous chapter ended with a melodramatic indication of the change that improved technology and connectivity will bring to training. It is hardly surprising that people involved in managing or delivering training feel ill at ease. We are at the stage where there is a recognition of the magnitude of the change but uncertainty about the appropriate initial response.

So far the changes brought about by the connected economy have affected economic and business activity. To use the accepted terminology, these have been business-to-business (B2B) or business-to-consumer (B2C) transactions. Business-to-employee (B2E) changes, of which an improved approach to training is an example, have lagged behind. The fact that there are high-profile claims of a revolution to come hardly adds to the training manager's peace of mind.

For example, the following has been attributed to John T. Chambers, the chief executive officer of Cisco Systems:

> Education over the Internet is so big it's going to make e-mail look like a rounding error.

In its December 1999 issue, the US magazine *Entrepreneur* included e-learning in its 'most important hot list to date' of business ideas for 2000. (Somewhat depressingly for some of our profession, virtual human resources – the outsourcing of specialist skills – also appeared on the list.) It argued that classroom training is old school and that online training companies that offer Internet- and intranet-based training are destined to be the new high achievers.[1]

There is no need, however, for those responsible for training to stare at the new technology systems like a snake at a mongoose – recognising that serious problems lie ahead but fearful to move. What is required is, first, a realistic assessment of the current position, and subsequently, the preparation of an appropriate agenda. It should be recognised that more general competitive and social forces are affecting the role of training in organisations (irrespective of technology). These forces will be considered briefly in the next section. Subsequently, this chapter will examine the changes in training in organisations. It will concentrate mainly on the developments that are occurring as a direct result of the new technology. To what extent have new systems become embedded? What is best practice? What can we learn from the US experience where applications are more advanced?

People as a source of competitive advantage

‘Training may be entering a new age with growing respect for the importance of the function’

Irrespective of the disruption caused by connectivity, training in organisations is in a state of transition. For some optimistic commentators this transition is all to the good: it may amount to a renaissance. Training may be entering a new age with growing respect for the importance of the function. At the heart of this optimistic perspective is recognition that the new basis of competition creates an opportunity: this can be paraphrased as ‘people are a source of competitive advantage’. Some other influences on the changing role of training (and the dilemmas they create) must also be recognised and their impact considered.

Few employees in modern corporations have not at some time or other been on the receiving end of an announcement that ‘people are our most important asset’. Inevitable cynicism has followed from the downsizing and ‘involuntary redundancy’ of the 1990s: if people are the most important asset, they can scarcely be regarded as a fixed asset!

Despite this cynicism, there is a powerful argument that economic forces have swung the balance in favour of the capable employee who can bring skills to the organisation. These staff need to be encouraged, supported and valued if they are to be retained by the organisation. It is a matter for debate how this should be done – what are the most effective human resource policies under these circumstances? Focus Point 8 summarises one expression that has received particular prominence: the war for talent.

Focus Point 8: The war for talent

In 1998 the management consultancy McKinsey produced an article in its quarterly magazine that received considerable acclaim in the human resource profession.[2]

Following a comprehensive study of 77 corporations and more than 6,000 executives, McKinsey argued that the best talent will be harder to find and more difficult to keep.

There will be a 'war for talent' since:

> Superior talent will be tomorrow's prime source of competitive advantage. Any company seeking to exploit it must instill a talent mindset throughout the organization, starting at the top. (p48)

Large companies face some considerable challenges:

> A more complex economy demands a sophisticated talent with global acumen, multicultural influences, technological literacy, entrepreneurial skills, and the ability to manage increasingly de-layered, disaggregated organizations. (p47)

Moreover, small and medium-sized companies are targeting the same people sought by large companies and job mobility is increasing.

To win the 'war for talent', organisations must elevate talent management as a burning corporate priority:

> To attract and retain the people you need, you must create and perpetually refine an employee value proposition: senior management's answer to why a smart, energetic, ambitious individual would want to come and work with you rather than the team next door. That done, you must turn your attention to how you are going to recruit great talent and finally develop, develop, develop! (p46)

[Reproduced with permission from McKinsey.]

Important social questions may arise on the position of those people who do not have these valuable skills. How can we ensure that they are not excluded from the personal prosperity and self-esteem that results from good employment?

What, however, is generally accepted is that the new basis of competition has led to a new approach to competitive strategy. Globalisation, the growing awareness of consumers, the deregulation/liberalisation of trade and, above all, the communication revolution described as connectivity, have already been recognised as self-reinforcing drivers of change. The focus of business strategy has shifted away from narrow economics (being in the right market and operating with the appropriate cost structure) to a perspective based on maximising the resources of the organisation – particularly the human resources.

Two concepts are of key importance to understand what is happening in training. The first is the emergence of resource-based strategy: this is outlined in Focus Point 9.

The second key concept is that of the knowledge worker. The emergence of and importance of the activity of knowledge management will be considered further in Chapter 3. At this stage a knowledge worker can be described as someone whose work is intellectual in context; the task of knowledge workers is to share ideas and information and to bring value to the client or customer. To achieve this objective they must gain maximum advantage from information systems. Competition in the modern age, therefore, is not about metal-bashing or seeking to be the lowest-cost producer; it is about harnessing the creative talents in the organisation to bring value to existing and future clients.

Influences and dilemmas

Resource-based strategy offers a useful expression of the new opportunity for competition through people. Many of these people should properly be described as knowledge workers. In addition, there are a number of critical influences and dilemmas that shape the environment in which the training manager operates. The opportunities, influences and dilemmas are summarised in Figure 2. These were developed in the author's previous work.[3]

Focus Point 9: Resource-based strategy

In resource-based approaches to strategy, the emphasis is on using what a company can do rather than on where a company is currently positioned in the marketplace. Organisational strengths are developed, stretched, extended and leveraged for competitive advantage.

John Kay, the former director of the Said Business School at Oxford University, has described the importance of resource-based strategy in the following terms.[4]

Resource-based strategy:

> examines the dynamics of the successes and failures of firms by reference to their distinctive capabilities – the factors, often implicit and intangible, which differentiate them from their competitors in the same markets and which cannot be reproduced by these competitors even after the advantages they offer are recognized. (pvi)

Effective strategy must start from:

> what the company is distinctively good at, not from what it would like to be good at, and is adaptive and opportunistic in exploiting what is distinctive in these capabilities. (p43)

The main elements of resource-based strategy are as follows:

- Firms are essentially collections of capabilities.
- The effectiveness of a firm depends on the match between these capabilities and the market it serves.
- The growth, and appropriate boundaries, of a firm are limited by its capabilities.
- Some of these capabilities can be purchased or created and are available to all firms.
- Others are irreproducible, or reproducible only with substantial difficulty, by other firms, and it is on these that competitive advantage depends.
- Such capabilities are generally irreproducible because they are a product of the history of the firm or by virtue of uncertainty (even within the firm itself) about their nature (pp33–4).

John Kay places great value on resource-based strategy and indeed argues that the resource-based theory 'unifies most of what is substantial and significant in our existing knowledge of business behavior' (p33).

Figure 2

OPPORTUNITIES

The key source of competitive advantage is now embedded in the skills and capabilities of knowledge workers.

The new global economy reinforced by the information/telecommunications revolution and by regulation has changed the nature of competition.

Resource-based strategy shifts in competitive emphasis from an external response to market conditions to an internal response based on the development of internal capabilities.

CRITICAL INFLUENCES

Accomplished and marketable individuals seek employability – appropriate opportunities to develop their own capability in both the long and short term.

Technology permits new approaches to the delivery of training – particularly dispersed access across networks.

DILEMMAS

The need to maintain an appropriate balance between the requirements of the organisation and the demands of the individual.

Responsibility for the formulation of training policy and the management of its implementation has become diffuse:
- a co-ordinated approach is needed on developing advantage through people
- line managers carry more responsibility for developing their staff.

Targeting and monitoring of resource is more critical and more difficult:
- more people initiate training interventions
- much may be unco-ordinated/unrecorded.

(Taken from Sloman M. A Handbook for Training Strategy. 2nd edn. Aldershot, Gower, 1999.)

Key knowledge workers are often well aware of their own value. They have shifted their focus from employment to employability. The attractiveness of a career with a single organisation diminishes when it is recognised that most organisations have a shorter lifespan than the individual's span of post-education activity to retirement. As was recognised in the war for talent (Focus Point 8), job mobility is increasing. One major effect on training in organisations is the need to offer development opportunities: expressed at Ernst & Young as 'the place to grow'. A consequence (listed as a dilemma in Figure 2) is the need for the training manager to balance the requirements of the individual and organisation when allocating the resources devoted to training.

One other influence and two other dilemmas are identified in Figure 2. The first is the fact that technology permits new approaches to training: this will form the substance of this chapter. The two dilemmas emphasise the widening ownership of training organisations. First, there must be a recognition that responsibility for training has become more diffuse. In particular, line managers have been encouraged to carry more responsibility for the training requirements of their staff. Second, it is more difficult to manage training on the basis of a central control mechanism. Once devolution of responsibility is encouraged, so the monitoring of resources must become more difficult.

The impact of technology

‘Technology should be seen as a means, not as an end’

Competitive and social forces are therefore creating a new set of challenges for everyone who is concerned with effective training – irrespective of the opportunities offered by enhanced technologies. One of the central themes of this book is that technology should be seen as a means, not as an end. Undoubtedly it can offer those directly involved in managing or delivering training an opportunity to do their jobs more effectively. Taking the broader organisational perspective, a realistic awareness of the current state and application of the technology is a necessary precondition for an implementation strategy. The potential gains from the new technology are about much more than effective training delivery.

In the remainder of this chapter, an overview or mapping of the current state of e-learning will be offered. Just what is going on beyond the hype? This overview will be presented in the following sections. First, such indications as are available on the extent of implementation in the UK will be reviewed: one particular initiative, the corporate university, will be discussed in detail.

Attention will then switch to the experience of the USA. The work of the American Society for Training and Development and the independent commentator Elliott Masie will be considered in turn.

Finally, learning systems will be defined and analysed.

The growing interest

Any overview of the current UK position indicates considerable and growing interest in the potential of e-learning; so far, however, it has not become widely embedded in organisations.

In January 1999 the (then) Institute of Personnel and Development published its first survey of training and development in UK establishments. The second, of what is to become an annual series, was published in spring of the following year. The 2000 survey[5] revealed a positive repositioning of training:

> Current optimism about the performance of the UK's economy is reflected in managements' apparent increased commitment to training. A larger proportion of establishments than last year have a training budget, and over half of all respondents expect to increase their investment in training over the next 12 months. (p1)

And:

> One of the most significant issues facing establishments over the next two or three years will be the need to ensure that training is more closely aimed with business strategy ... Nearly half of all respondents have integrated their training strategies with their business strategies....

One of the key sections of the IPD survey concerned training methods and delivery. Here the conclusions were:

> While the majority of establishments continue to rely on traditional techniques for delivering training, there has been a rapid expansion in the use of the new electronic technologies over the past 12 months. (p2)

The first IPD survey in 1999 suggested that new forms of electronic technology described as training via the Internet/intranets and (in an even smaller number of cases) the extranet had penetrated only about a quarter of the establishments. However, respondents said that they expected their use of these electronic techniques to increase and these expectations had been realised a year later.

By 2000, the relative growth of new technology as a delivery mechanism was far greater than the other forms of training techniques categorised in the survey (on-the-job, face-to-face and formal education, for example). The survey was able to postulate:

> New technology is starting to become embedded in the workplace and is already playing an important role in delivering training in many UK establishments, although it has some way to go before it is universally accepted. (p8)

The IPD's survey was a most useful addition to our knowledge of the UK training environment. As far as technology training is concerned, it reflected the mood of the moment: most importantly it saw the contribution of technology-based training primarily in terms of a new channel for delivery. This view was shared by other commentators/authors at the time.

The interactive learning company Xebec McGraw-Hill also undertakes an annual survey. This sample is drawn from the readership of *Training* magazine and Xebec's own database. As such it represents a group that can be assumed to be more aware of the potential of technology than the population of training managers in general. The broad conclusions are of interest and consistent with the general pattern. The 2000 survey showed that 80 per cent of organisations have a corporate intranet, but less than 30 per cent were using it to deliver online training. Disappointingly, only 39 per cent of those delivering training online rated it as successful – which was said to illustrate the difficulty of overcoming the cultural issues. However, almost 80 per cent of all respondents believed that online learning (the term used in the survey) will ultimately prove successful.

Despite these and other surveys, it is hard to be certain of the extent to which technology-based training has been embraced across the board in the UK. First, there is a general problem of measurement. What is meant by 'proportion of training' type figures? Is it defined by the number of users, number of events or number of hours? To date no standard terminology has emerged. This fact should also be borne in mind when considering the information contained in later sections.

A second point concerns vendor activity. Attempts to get a clear perspective are not always assisted by hype from suppliers of systems. It is in their interests to present a picture in which there is a flurry of activity, with leading-edge companies in the vanguard. If this message were to be accepted, there would be great pressure on the laggards.

Such information as is available suggests a far less clear picture. Undoubtedly, some large organisations have found that, provided it is given sufficient resources, a commitment to technology-based training works for them. Others appear to be biding their time or are simply unaware or uninterested.

The corporate university

Several of the leading organisations in the UK have committed their resources in the form of a corporate university. These received what amounted to an official endorsement from the Government in 2000 in the form of a publication from the Department of Industry. Further information is set out in Focus Point 10 where the concept is defined.

Corporate universities have received a great deal of attention and may offer an attractive way forward in the right circumstances. However, the concept should not be embraced without some critical analysis. Cynically, it could be suggested that (with the exception of accreditation of programmes) a corporate university could be no more than:

✐ a more modern manifestation of the traditional staff college – the residential industry training establishments that were so fashionable in the 1970s and 1980s

Focus Point 10: Corporate universities

In 2000, the Department of Trade and Industry in conjunction with the Department for Education and Employment, the Campaign for Learning and the Further Education Development Agency, published 'The future of corporate learning'.[6]

The publication falls within the tradition of attempts to improve training in the UK by analysing and advocating best practice. Although the publication did not specifically advocate the establishment of corporate universities, by giving them a prominent focus it implicitly endorsed the idea:

> Recently, increasing numbers of British businesses have also felt the need to create new institutions called corporate universities. The past two or three years have seen a particular growth in this trend, and as a result, there are now well over 20 initiatives that might be described as corporate universities, from Unipart U – one of the longest-established – to the BT Academy, launched earlier this year. It is clear that this trend is set to continue with more and more businesses considering whether this will be the best approach to put people at the heart of their business. (p7)

Two definitions of corporate universities were offered in the report: the first from Henley Management College and the second from the publication by the Campaign for Learning.

> A corporate university is formed when a corporation seeks to relate its training and development strategies to its business strategy by co-ordination and integration and by the development of intellectual capital within the organisation in pursuit of its corporate aims and objectives.

> A corporate university is an internal structure designed to improve individual and business performance by ensuring that the learning and knowledge of a corporation is directly connected to its business strategy. A corporate university's students are drawn from its employees. It has the capacity to offer formal accreditation for some of the learning it provides. (p7)

The corporate university movement, like many initiatives in learning and development, has its origins in the USA. A useful reference site is the Corporate University Xchange (www.corpu.com).

According to the Xchange there were over 2,000 corporate universities in the USA (up from 400 in 1986). Of the Fortune 500 companies, 40 per cent have invested in a corporate university. The average cost is 2 per cent of the company's payroll.

✐ a rebadging and re-promotion of a company's internal training department.

‹A healthy scepticism is a vital attribute at this time of transition›

There is a grain of truth in such a view – a healthy scepticism is a vital attribute of the observer's armoury at this time of transition. Certainly, the corporate university is an attractive option for only the more confident organisation.

However, there is considerable merit in exploring a feature of many corporate universities. This is the opportunity for greater collaboration between the educational establishment and the corporate organisation. Such collaboration can of course take place much more easily in the connected economy. The Cap Gemini Ernst & Young Virtual Business School, which is the subject of the case study presented at the end of this chapter, offers an illustration.

Broader opportunities beyond delivery

Corporate universities are a leading-edge exception, not the norm. The predominant message from the available evidence is that there is an expansion in technology-based training, but that its penetration is restricted to a small number of organisations that are wrestling with the practical issues surrounding its use.

This section returns to a more general aspect of the impact of technology and the position of e-learning.

In Chapter 1 (page 4), one of the more important implications of operating in the connected economy was expressed in the following terms. Arguments on the appropriate platform for technology-based training are over. Training will be delivered through the Internet/intranet using web-based protocols. The term e-learning (as a shorthand for e-learning and e-training) was adopted as the preferred term to describe this development. A brief outline of the early developments in technology-based training is set out in Focus Point 11.

Focus Point 11: Emergence of technology-based training (TBT)[7]

TBT can be said to have emerged in the 1970s when the emphasis was placed on computer-assisted learning using mainframe computers. A National Development Programme in Computer Assisted Learning (NDPCAL) was in existence between 1970 and 1974. Also in the mid-1970s, Barclaycard introduced an extensive computer-assisted training programme for its data entry staff.

In the 1980s developments in computers gave an enhanced structure to TBT. The micro-computer emerged; graphics and colour could be introduced to programmes. A national computer-based training forum was established in 1982 with the support of the National Computer Centre. The Government (in the form of the Manpower Services Commission) established a project (Project 'Author') in 1983–4 to encourage the spread of the approach. New products in the form of laser disks and interactive video appeared.

In the 1990s the widespread use of personal computers (and later laptop computers) meant that the CD-ROM (compact disk read-only memory: a form of high-capacity storage using laser optics rather than magnetic means to read data) emerged as a powerful form for distributing training material. The storage capacity available permitted data to be presented in a multimedia context.

This terminology provides a useful background to emphasise a feature of the current training scene. Much of the thinking and analysis has taken place within the following mindset: technology-based training is solely (or at least mainly) about new improved channels for delivery using the intranet. This is an understandable mistake, but a mistake nonetheless. The opportunities for delivering more effective training that have arisen through technology, and connectivity, extend far beyond delivery.

The perception that technology-based training is solely about improved delivery channels may disappear as the market develops. Connectivity and the blurring of boundaries are going to have a significant impact as will 'new unforeseen developments' to use Clayton Christensen's phrase.

An example taken from an ongoing debate in higher education will provide a useful illustration. In 2000 the Committee of Vice Chancellors and Principals of the UK Universities (CVCP) and the Higher Education Funding Council for England (HEFCE) produced a joint report. This sought to map the changes affecting the new world of global higher education and to suggest how they may impact on British universities. Much of the discussion was on the emerging corporate university movement. However, the broader focus was indicated in the choice of title: 'The business of borderless education'. The CVCP report recognised that corporate universities place increasing emphasis on the use of technology to deliver training. This was only a part of the picture that needed to be considered. The whole market was changing with new suppliers (often media companies, including publishers) entering sectors traditionally occupied by non-profit-making, publicly funded universities. Further, teaching and learning would be affected in a number of obvious and less obvious ways:

> Teaching and learning in the borderless context is a hybrid of existing modes. In distance learning currently paper-based delivery is still more common than virtual approaches. The scene is one of increasing complexity with a convergence of face-to-face and distance learning approaches. A shift towards treating students as 'customers' or 'clients' is also becoming more pronounced, particularly in relation to the working adult market. . .

> The craft tradition that saw individual academics responsible for the development and delivery of a course is under pressure from a more industrial model where discrete elements (such as subject knowledge, pedagogical expertise, multimedia skills, assessment techniques) are drawn together within course teams of individuals with specific roles. For advocates of the new forms of provision the decline of the cottage industry approach adopted by universities to teaching and learning may be a matter for celebration; however, for many academic staff fundamental questions emerge about key educational processes and values.[8] (p15)

As the report indicates, the change is profound. It is more than better technology offering improved delivery. It is about the development of borderless learning and education. This, indeed, is the message of blur (see pages 12–13).

Developments in the USA: the work of the ASTD

Not only is implementation more advanced in the USA, its trainers have developed a different approach from the profession in the UK. Training is not seen as such an integral part of human resources, and to an extent has developed as a separate discipline based on the concept of instructional development and design. The implications of this approach will be considered later in this book, especially in Chapter 6 where the new skills required by the trainer will be reconsidered. In addition, the USA is a large geographically dispersed economy that is the home of the world's leading software companies. Together, these elements have two important implications:

- The spread of e-learning has been more extensive.
- There is a greater awareness of the wider gains from technology – extending beyond e-learning delivery.

There is no shortage of information available on developments in the USA. An especially useful service is offered by the American Society for Training and Development (ASTD), which is a membership organisation providing a regular output of reports. Its website is www.astd.org.

Each year the ASTD produces a State of the Industry Report. Given the reporting lag, it generally refers to statistical information on activities up to two years earlier. The 1999 report contained a feature by Laurie J. Bassi and Mark E. Van Buren on training trends.[9] The section on delivery methods considered practices in leading-edge firms. In part these firms were selected by their approach to training delivery.

For these organisations, instructor-led classroom training as a percentage of total training is declining and predicted to continue to decline. Bassi and Van Buren's feature estimated that it could drop to 60 per cent of total delivery. In 2000, to be considered leading-edge, an organisation would have to deliver more than a quarter of training using learning technologies (the term preferred in the feature):

> Several technologies in particular are leading the way ... By the year 2000, 80 per cent expect to be using CD-ROMs; intranets (70 per cent) and the Internet (58 per cent) ranked second and third. In fact,

both forms of web-based training are projected to triple in use between 1997 and 2000.[9] (p7)

The feature comes to a clear conclusion:

> The leading learning technology by the year 2000 is expected to be the company intranet. The typical organisation expects to use its intranet to deliver more than 22 per cent of its sources by that time.[9] (p7)

One other particularly relevant observation of the feature was the following comment:

> The percentage of courses that leading-edge firms deliver via learning technologies are not any higher than in the typical organization.

> In fact for some technologies, such as CD-ROMs and the Internet, the leading-edge percentages are lower. In other words, to join the leading edge, your organisation won't have to use the technologies you currently have for more courses. Rather you'll have a greater variety of learning technologies to deliver your training than you currently do.[9] (p7)

On this basis, the following seem to be the main lessons to be drawn from the ASTD analysis:

- ✍ There will be a shift away from traditional instructor-led, classroom training, which will affect *both* the ways in which training is delivered and the way people learn.
- ✍ In the short term (perhaps three to five years), the company intranet will be the most important vehicle for delivery.
- ✍ In the short term, about a quarter of training will be delivered using learning technology.

From the UK perspective, 'what happens over there will happen over here in time' is likely to apply to learning technology. However, a word of warning is necessary. The subsequent (and latest) survey available from the ASTD showed that there had been a levelling off in the use of learning technologies. To quote from a summary commentary on the 2000 report:[10]

> Last year's report showed that the average Benchmarking Service firm delivered 77.6 per cent of its training in a classroom setting and 9.1 per cent via learning technologies. In this year's survey, these figures changed very little, with the percentage of training delivered via

classrooms up to 78.5 per cent and technology-delivered training, actually dropping slightly to 8.5 per cent. (p15)

While this is not likely to be significant in statistical terms, it suggests a plateau rather than the continued growth forecast earlier. There is a reporting lag: the figures relate to 1998. However, given the increases in the growth of learning technology reported earlier, this does raise questions. The ASTD feels that growth will continue, and its 2000 report suggested the following reasons for the plateau in growth:

> This levelling off in the growth of learning technologies suggests that perhaps organizations are finding technology-based training difficult to do well. Challenges that companies may be facing include technological barriers, cultural resistance to a new way of learning, and the challenge of ensuring that technology-based training is cost-effective and produces results that truly enhance individual and firm performance.

> Nevertheless, there is no doubt that organizations are making tremendous investments in learning technologies and that these investments will continue to grow.[10] (p15)

This finding is important. The platform is available; implementation may become a critical issue.

Another significant contribution from the ASTD concerns its review of potential development in learning technologies. A useful 1999 report entitled 'Trendz' appeared as a supplement in its regular magazine. Some extracts are set out in Focus Point 12 and serve to emphasise the rich environment that will emerge.

Focus Point 12 may indicate the shape of things to come. However, what can be delivered on the current platforms is more than enough to make all those with responsibility for training very excited. Current multimedia training (whether delivered through CD-ROM or the intranet) can incorporate three-dimensional graphics animation, a choice of decisions in scenarios, and routing options that allow the learner to navigate his or her own path through the module.

One phrase that is entering the vocabulary is 'high touch'. This is the use of leading-edge technology to replicate the softer interaction that

Focus Point 12: A glimpse of future trends

In November 1999 the American Society for Training and Development (ASTD) produced a special supplement to its magazine.[11] This supplement sought to identify trends that were most likely to change the way that trainers worked. In its own words, the ASTD sorted through 'mountains of predictions, opinions and guesses about the future of learning and work'. Some of the trends that could affect technology and training were suggested by Jay Cross, information architect of Internet Time Group (www.internettime.com). He stated that the following will emerge 'in our not too distant training future':

- personal software agents that crawl the Web to screen and feed information to personal portals
- connected gadgets and gizmos that simplify (and complicate) our lives
- plug-and-play training modularity
- learning standards that create interchangeable, Lego-like objects that slash costs and development time
- personal files and programs that run directly from the Internet.

Elsewhere in the supplement, according to the ASTD:

> A new breed of technology is heading the pack and aiming to quell criticism of online learning as a static, isolating experience. In fact, it encompasses several technologies that connect online learners and the instructor in a virtual classroom. Synchronous online learning is already available at a fraction of the cost of higher-end video-conferencing systems.
>
> Adding synchronous voice capabilities is the first hurdle. Existing systems that rely on teleconferencing technology are being joined by new technology, voice-over Internet protocol (VOIP) that allows real-time voice transmission over the same data pipes that carry online learning.
>
> The addition of synchronous voice capabilities to online learning is only a stepping stone to the real objective – IP (Internet protocol)-based audio/video. Technologies such as VOIP will lead to low-cost solutions.[11] (p34)

(Synchronous describes the situation when individuals are all interacting in the same, real time. See Focus Point 18, page 115 for a fuller definition.)

Reproduced with permission from the American Society for Training and Development, with thanks to Pat Galagan, Editor-in-Chief, Training and Development.

comes with a one-to-one exchange with the tutor. High touch reflects an aspiration that this can be achieved. However, it is tempting to become entranced with the vehicle and to forget the objective of more effective training and enhanced learning. This is summarised in Proposition 4.

Proposition 4

There is a danger of becoming seduced by the functionality of the technology, rather than concentrating on its use.

Developments in the USA: the work of Elliott Masie

The sentiments outlined in Proposition 4 would doubtless command the support of Elliott Masie. Described as a technology and learning futurist, he has established the Masie Center to consider how organisations can absorb technology and create continuous learning and knowledge internally. The centre (www.masie.com) produces an interactive newsletter (*Learning Decisions*) supported by regular online updates (www.learningdecisions.com).

Masie has a number of attributes that make his analysis worthy of the attention of training managers. First, he is not associated with any vendor or manufacturer of learning technology. He is 'learning-system-neutral'. Second, he is not seduced by the technology: he places his attention firmly on the learner and technology is seen as the means to an end.

‹ e-learning is not about computers and is not about computing ›

He argues that the 'e', as in e-learning, should be an abbreviation for experience, not electronic. The learner should be the focus. E-learning is not about computers and is not about computing. It should be about communications with the learner, seeking to increase knowledge and encouraging meaningful interchanges and transactions that achieve these objectives.

Masie argues that our current stage in e-learning carries high risk. Doubtless some experiments will fail. The new learning techniques, if exploited effectively, can offer huge advantages to the learner. Knowledge can be adapted and disseminated instantly, for example; 'timeshifting' is possible, by which people can learn at the time that is most suitable for them.

Masie's philosophy and approach is entirely compatible with the messages contained in this book. His newsletter contains frequent analyses of the key issues in the learning technology – seen from the prospect of those implementing systems in the organisation. This frequently allows him to promote a useful terminology of learning technology. Illustrations are shown in Focus Point 13.

Focus Point 13: Elliott Masie's terminology

Some illustrations:

Learning portals

Learning portals are popping up in a wide variety of flavours, all focusing on building a single doorway or entrance to learning services (online and classroom); providing a learning architecture including training management technology; creating an access point to the training/learning department; and providing online communication and collaboration capabilities to learners.

It makes sense, on many levels. If we can create a simpler way for training professionals or learners to access critical resources, it is a win! If we can help learners make better learning choices, it is a win! If we can provide a simple way for organisations to access the capabilities of learning collaboration or training management systems through a portal site, it is a win!

(From Learning Decisions, February 2000)

Digital surround

The recipe for a Digital Surround is quite simple. Take a traditional instructor-led, classroom-based training experience and enhance the offering by adding technology before, during and after the in-person meeting. Digital Surrounds are the place where e-learning is spreading most quickly with organizations and where some of the bigggest returns on investment can be accomplished quickly.

(From Learning Decisions, March 2000)

Masie positions himself firmly on the side of the learner and is sympathetic to the training manager's day-to-day problems. He is good at articulating the benefits of learning technology, and the concept of a digital surround (see Focus Point 13) is particularly attractive. His concept of supporting training before, during and after the in-person meeting, coupled with the shift away from the classroom and instructor-led training, introduces the next proposition.

Proposition 5

Training will move from events to interventions.

Irrespective of the introduction of e-learning, the tendency has been for the delivery of training in more readily available chunks. Modularisation (delivering information in smaller segments) has become a popular theme as classroom events have been shorter in duration; e-learning can assist in this process and assist in making a reality of a prevalent trainer's soundbite: we must shift from 'just in case' training to 'just in time'.

E-learning systems

The final section of this chapter offers an attempt to map what will be described as a learning system. A learning system can be described as a multi-faceted software package that provides an e-learning solution. There is a booming market in the development of such systems, fuelled by venture capital companies anxious to reap the benefits from the new technological opportunities. A new industry of vendors of such systems has emerged. Their activities have dictated much of the professional agenda.

CIPD exhibitions for years to come will witness the arrival of new suppliers of systems. Many have emerged from multimedia companies who have built more sophisticated products and offered them through new delivery channels. Others have their genesis in software houses. Others are joint ventures.

Undoubtedly these vendors are making a positive contribution by increasing awareness of the potential gains from e-learning. There is nothing wrong with a supply-side initiative. Markets are not all demand-led. If they were, we would still be using carbon paper rather than the undesired (at the time) invention called the photocopier. The problems with new hitherto unimagined products generated from technological breakthroughs is that you cannot imagine them until you have seen them.

Everyone who is concerned with effective training must, however, retain primary focus on the needs of the learner. Proposition 4 (see page 42) should be committed to memory. Keeping a watchful eye on developments in learning systems is part of that process.

Figure 3 is meant to assist in understanding the functions that can be delivered by a learning system. It is entitled 'hard' technology to distinguish it from a similar mapping based in the softer aspects of implementation, which will be introduced in Chapter 6.

Figure 3
E-LEARNNG SYSTEM ARCHITECTURE

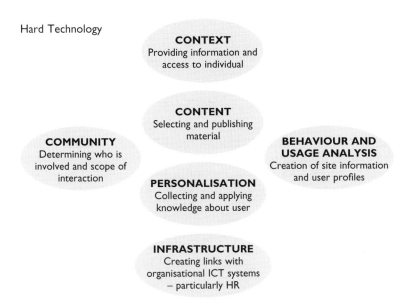

Hard Technology

CONTEXT
Providing information and access to individual

CONTENT
Selecting and publishing material

COMMUNITY
Determining who is involved and scope of interaction

BEHAVIOUR AND USAGE ANALYSIS
Creation of site information and user profiles

PERSONALISATION
Collecting and applying knowledge about user

INFRASTRUCTURE
Creating links with organisational ICT systems – particularly HR

The headings used in the bubbles of Figure 3 should become clearer in the context of the case studies developed in Chapter 4. However, the following definitions may assist.

   ✍ *Context* – this is about the style of the learning portal (see Focus Point 13, page 43, for Elliott Masie's definition). What sort of information does the individual receive on entry and to what extent is it customised for the organisation and individual?

   ✍ *Content* – this is the material that is made available to the learner through the system. Some systems are 'content agnostic' – they manage content generated elsewhere. Other systems are linked to particular suppliers of content or have made arrangements (often in the form of alliances) with providers of training materials (business schools or management consultancies).

   ✍ *Personalisation* – is the system capable of customisation to the individual learner's own requirements? This extends beyond the design of the portal – it is about adapting the individual information and learning needs.

   ✍ *Community* – who is involved in using the system? Is it purely internal staff? Is it global? Are outside organisers (suppliers, external consultants and academics) given access rights and can they participate?

   ✍ *Behaviour and usage analysis* – has the system a recording process that allows the organisation to collect the statistics needed to determine usage by predetermined organisational segments? Can individual use be monitored?

   ✍ *Infrastructure* – this concerns the link with other organisational IT systems. How does it relate to training records and recording and any billing or charging system? What is the link with performance management systems?

Some of these headings (Personalisation is an obvious example) will be features of the future development in learning systems rather than current packages. Nevertheless, as a review of the systems demonstrated at training conferences will indicate, all are available in some existing technology. Irrespective of current purchasing intentions, developments in the market for e-learning must be of interest to the trainer.

Taking into account all of these innovations, all those involved in training can look forward to an exhilarating future. Progress to date has not always been easy – as the case studies to be introduced in later chapters will illustrate. However, all the evidence is that technology will not be an inhibitor.

To date our technology has not been developed for learning purposes. Training managers have been obliged to take advantage of developments (for example, the company intranet) that were introduced for wider organisational/commercial purposes. Now technological barriers are diminishing. Many of the hurdles to e-learning, such as lack of interactivity, content availability, technological standards and bandwidth are currently being addressed. Given these circumstances two general points can be made. First, and this has been the main continuing theme of this chapter, the change will be profound and will extend beyond enhanced delivery. Second, there is a likelihood that a whole new approach to training and learning will be required as a consequence What form this could take will be considered in the next chapter.

References

1   Reproduced with permission of *Entrepreneur*, December 1999. (www.entrepreneur.com.)

2   CHAMBERS E. G., FOULON M., HANDFIELD-JONES H., HANKIN S. M. *and* MICHAELS E. G. III 'The war for talent'. *The McKinsey Quarterly*. 1998. pp44–57 (www.mckinsey.com).

3   SLOMAN M. *A Handbook for Training Strategy*. 2nd edn. Aldershot, Gower, 1999.

4   KAY J. *The Business of Economics*. Oxford, Oxford University Press, 1996.

5   *Training and Development in Britain 2000*. London, Institute of Personnel and Development, 2000.

6   Department for Education and Employment, the Campaign for Learning and the Further Education Development Agency, 'The future of corporate learning'. London, Department of Trade and Industry, 2000.

7   The analysis in Table 11 was drawn from a paper presented by Judith Christian-Carter of Effective Learning Services at the IPD's TechTraining 1999 Forum. I am grateful for her permission to reproduce her work.

8   'The business of borderless education'. *UK Perspectives: Summary Report*. London, CVCP, 2000.

9   BASSI L. J. *and* VAN BUREN M. E. *Sharpening the Leading Edge: The ASTD state of industry report*. Alexandria, Va., ASTD, 1999.

10   McMurrer D. P., Van Buren M. E. *and* Woodwell W. H. Jr
     The ASTD 2000 State of Industry Report. Alexandria, Va., ASTD,
     2000.

11   Abernathy D., Allerton H., Barron T. *and* Salopek J.,
     'Trendz'. *Training and Development*. November 1999.

Case Study

CAP GEMINI ERNST & YOUNG VIRTUAL BUSINESS SCHOOL

Background

Cap Gemini Ernst & Young UK Ltd was created in May 2000 from the merger of the former management consultancy practice of Ernst & Young with Cap Gemini and Gemini Consulting. The new organisation has an impressive list of clients and provides management and solutions consultancy across all sectors of industry, including energy, finance, technology, manufacturing, transport and government services.

Cap Gemini Ernst & Young employs around 1,000 consulting and support staff in the UK. The majority of these staff are based in the London head office, although many of the consultants work at client sites for lengthy periods of time.

The Virtual Business School (VBS) was launched in October 1998 by Ernst & Young's management consultancy and was seen at the time as:

> a way of providing consultants with a range of innovative learning experiences which would address significant gaps in their development, as well as providing a framework within which management consultancy services could create rich and valuable knowledge.

The concept of the VBS emerged out of three broad objectives:

✎ to introduce a greater knowledge/content dimension into learning within the management consultancy practice (building on and complementing the technical, methodological and personal development programmes that already existed)

$\mathscr{E}$ to provide consultants with a new and different learning opportunity to give them a sense that the company was a place where access to sources of learning and knowledge exist to enhance their own capabilities

$\mathscr{E}$ to create a corporate university that was more than simply 'rebadging' the training department (a common criticism of the corporate university movement), and in doing so, make a public demonstration of the company's commitment to the quality and innovativeness of learning and development within CGEY relative to other professional service firms.

In order to create a working VBS, an alliance was formed with Henley Management College. Henley was chosen out of eight shortlisted business schools because it was seen to be flexible in its approach and because of its commitment to and understanding of the VBS concept. Indeed, a common vision was apparent between the two entities. These concerned changing the face of business education through business-to-business school connectivity, leading ultimately to the blurring of the physical boundaries between different universities and the creation of a new system of learning providers.

The Virtual Business School centres

Due to the 'virtual' nature of the VBS, its form and substance will evolve to reflect the needs of the individual as well as the needs of the business. The VBS currently has four virtual centres that act as a focus and an operating framework. Typically, each centre develops learning programmes, events and activities that:

$\mathscr{E}$ are demand-led and respond to learning needs

$\mathscr{E}$ have a specific knowledge-creation dimension, such as a specific piece of research

$\mathscr{E}$ are extended programmes of education and development leading to the award of a qualification, such as an MBA.

The work of the VBS centres is ultimately to:

$\mathscr{E}$ develop and offer accredited and relevant educational programmes within the company leading to, for example, MBAs and doctorates

✐ exploit leading-edge remote-learning technologies, such as 'connected classrooms' and training via the Internet

✐ open a gateway to the wider business school, learning and knowledge-rich communities

✐ provide forums where insights and ideas can be shared and developed between staff members from the company and Henley faculty staff, in some cases leading to joint research projects, publications and/or conferences.

The following 'centres' were constructed to allow a platform for learning to be established.

1 The centre for postgraduate learning
The centre for postgraduate learning develops a range of education programmes that will lead to the award of a recognised external qualification. These may include a doctoral programme and a master's degree in consulting.

At present, some 16 CGEY staff are studying for the MBA. This is viewed as a 'challenging programme which requires considerable personal investment in terms of time, money and effort'.

2 The centre for leadership development
This centre is seen as an informal and indirect means of learning. It concerns itself with 'developing learning solutions which increase the leadership capability of the company'. The main purpose of the centre is to develop learning solutions that increase leadership profile, capability and performance. Approximately every six weeks, staff members attend a seminar. These sessions are demand-led by the business and focus on relevant topics (either technically or of general relevance), such as emotional intelligence and corporate stories.

3 The centre for research and innovation
This is seen as possibly the most powerful centre and often generates outside interest. It can be said that this centre is influenced greatly by corporate culture and is ultimately driven by client and business needs.

Staff members are given the opportunity to undertake applied research projects (by means of MBA assignments, doctoral theses, joint research papers and published articles). In addition, in some cases sponsorship is given by the company for other individuals to undertake research on its behalf. By using applied research methods, intellectual capital is increased and value given to the business by means of the enhancement of thought leadership.

4 The centre for connected learning

This was initially set up as a discussion site consisting of forums where individuals could share knowledge. The resource investment for this centre was initially very low because it was dependent on the knowledge of forum members. However, this centre has developed to a powerful site of connected learning.

This centre is not viewed as a stand-alone centre but as part of an infrastructure capable of supporting other types of centre. A pilot has been created as a virtual business simulation game whereby virtual teams are created that can be cross-cultural or from different offices. These teams are required to operate as a 'virtual' business facing the same type of issue, as in reality.

This pilot produced positive results and the centre is seen to be capable of supporting strategy and cross-cultural virtual team-working.

The challenges for the future

Challenges facing the Virtual Business School concern the degree of connectivity of the organisation, management of the centres and motivation of staff. If expansion of the VBS is to be fruitful, it must be easily accessed by staff members.

Motivation of staff is a key challenge, but this applies to all other forms of learning. Staff members must see value being added to the organisation and accept this form of technology if this form of learning is to be successful. Management of the VBS is also central to its success. Discussion groups will need moderating. This issue has been highlighted in a working paper from Henley Management College.

However, the greatest challenge facing the VBS is the issue of content. How is it possible to tailor the content to individual needs? E-learning is more effective for disseminating technical information. Using e-learning for skills such as influencing is more difficult unless the use of interactivity is promoted to increase self-awareness among participants.

Generally, the key to the future success of the VBS is the exploitation of all available technology to create a fully connected learning centre.

Chapter 3

A new paradigm
for training

We made too many wrong mistakes

The previous two chapters have set the context in which the training will be delivered in the organisation of the future. Chapter 1 considered how connectivity has altered the basis of competition; Chapter 2 summarised the consequent developments in training.

Before we consider how those who carry responsibility for training can build their own practical agenda, one further stage in the argument must be presented. This is the view that the changes that have arisen from connectivity have been so far-reaching that they demand a completely new conceptual approach to training in organisations: the view that they demand a new paradigm.

Paradigms, models and frameworks

One of the Chambers dictionary definitions of a paradigm is: 'a basic theory, a conceptual framework within which scientific theories are constructed'.

A change in a paradigm (popularly described as a paradigm shift) is important and exciting. It offers different ways of thinking that open up new practical possibilities.

An historical example is the shift that took place when the realisation grew that the world was round, not flat. This affected a whole range of perceptions, thoughts and ideas from the abstract to the practical. When people disappeared without trace, they were no longer thought to have fallen off the end of the Earth!

A change or shift in a paradigm will have an impact on a whole range of constructs and ideas that apply across different situations and activities. It will necessitate the development of a different kind of framework or template to guide implementation in the organisation. Such frameworks will need to be redesigned in the context of the new paradigm. The frameworks available for training are considered in Chapter 4 (where the agenda for the organisation is considered), in Chapter 6 (where the role of the trainer is outlined) and in Chapter 7 (where the impact on the industry is discussed).

Learning and training

Two models have dominated our approach to training over the last two decades; they will be considered in turn below. At a crude level one can be described as a training model, the other as a learning model. Much of the recent debate and discussion in the literature has emphasised the primacy of learning over training: the job of human resource development is to encourage learning. Training, by impli-cation, is somewhat passé.

‘Despite the fact that it is no longer fashionable, training (as opposed to learning) is still a useful concept’

One of the arguments of this book is that despite the fact that it is no longer fashionable, training (as opposed to learning) is still a useful concept. This argument is expressed in Proposition 6.

Proposition 6

The distinction between learning and training is of value and should be maintained.

Initial definitions of terms were offered in Focus Point 4 (page 5). A further discussion on learning is offered in Chapter 5, where the cur-rent body of information on the learning process is reviewed. The important distinction is simply restated. Learning lies in the domain of the individual: it is about the process of changing patterns and behaviour. Training lies in the domain of the organisation: it is an intervention designed to improve the knowledge and skills of employees.

The following will illustrate the different domains. Some people who arrive in organisations learn rapidly where the limit and boundaries of acceptable behaviour lie. They learn, for example, to claim the maximum expenses. So far, however, there is no evidence of training intervention to support such behaviour. There are no courses available with titles like 'Augmenting your Expenses: An introduction' or 'Advanced Expense Augmentation (participants must have attended 'Augmenting your Expenses: An introduction')'. The organisation does not intervene in this way; some people, however, learn (in this case bad habits) from others.

Traditionally, organisational interventions that carried the label 'training' have tended to be directive – individuals have been told what to do and expected to do what they are told. Training course menus were published in the form of catalogues and individuals were expected to participate. Although times have changed, this still applies, for example, to professional training and training associated with qualifications.

Directive approaches are not without value in appropriate circumstances: health and safety would be an example. Generally, however, the modern economy has demanded more discretion, creativity, innovation and acceptance of responsibility from employees. This has resulted in a shift to a focus on learning and the learner. The mechanisms that can be used will be explored in Chapter 6 (pages 138–158). At this stage, it is sufficient to note that such mechanisms have included self-managed learning groups, the communication of learning systems or pathways, learning contracts and support through coaching and mentoring.

Systematic training

In the UK the systematic training model became increasingly accepted in the late 1960s as a result of the work of the industrial training boards. These bodies had the role of extending training throughout whole sectors of the economy and a common model was adopted. This is illustrated as Figure 4.

Figure 4

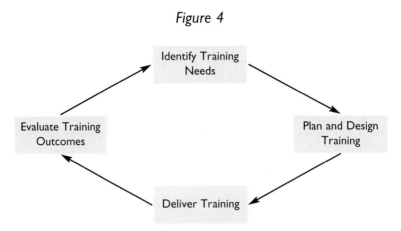

(National Standards for Training and Development © Crown Copyright 1992; reproduced by permission of the Training Development Lead Body)

It can be seen that the basis of this model is to divide a training intervention into a series of sequential steps or stages. The benefit of this model is that it focuses on the need to apply a systematic, disciplined approach to each stage in the process.

The model was firmly grounded in the scientific management of the 1960s and 1970s. A great deal of useful work was undertaken that built on the constructs of the model. Alternative techniques for needs identification and evaluation, for example, have been produced and promulgated. Various commentators have developed and extended the model, often by emphasising the importance of introducing feedback loops between the different stages.

The value of applying such a disciplined approach is at its greatest where the problem definition (ie the articulation of the training need) is clear and the population to be trained is clearly identifiable and large in number. In the USA a whole new discipline of instructional systems development (ISD) has been developed using a systematic approach. The emergence of a powerful new platform for training has given a whole new impetus for effective training design. There is therefore a great deal to be gained from revisiting the underlying ISD principles. Figure 5 is taken from a 1998 American Society for Training and Development report on the impact of learning technology as the activities undertaken by human resource

Figure 5

STEPS IN ISD AND LEARNING TECHNOLOGY IMPLEMENTATION PROCESS

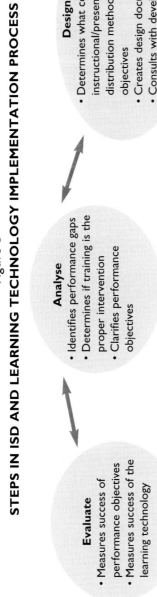

Design
- Determines what content instructional/presentation/distribution method will fulfill objectives
- Creates design document
- Consults with developer, evaluator and implementor

Analyse
- Identifies performance gaps
- Determines if training is the proper intervention
- Clarifies performance objectives

Develop
- Uses design document to create materials that are delivered via various presentation methods
- Consults with designer and implementor

Evaluate
- Measures success of performance objectives
- Measures success of the learning technology

Deliver
- Works with technical staff to set up and support learning technologies
- Works with suppliers
- Consults with designer and developer

(Reproduced by permission of the American Society for Training and Development[1])

professionals. It helpfully expresses the ISD model in terms of learning technology.[1]

Although of undoubted operational value, systematic training has deficiencies as a model. The most important of these is that, at its simplest, it treats a problem in isolation. The cycle is not embedded in any organisational context. It is the responsibility of the training professional, once the first indication of the training need emerges, to apply his or her toolkit (the systematic training model) to come up with an efficient solution. It is essentially a reactive process rather than a proactive one.

One competitive function of the training manager is to enable the organisation to become more effective. In part this must be achieved by proactively identifying and offering training interventions that improve the knowledge or skill base. This does not necessarily involve waiting until someone has identified a need. Taken in isolation, the systematic training model is unduly restrictive.

The learning organisation

> ‘ The learning organisation may be better seen as an aspirational intention ’

By contrast, the second important model – the learning organisation – is wide in scope and ambition. It encourages proactivity. It is a learning rather than a training model. Unfortunately, it is often uncertain in definition and difficult to see what it means in practice. The learning organisation may be better seen as an aspirational intention rather than as a practical framework for implementation.

Much of the early impetus came from the American organisational psychologist Chris Argyris, whose work has centered on developing individual potential within the company. In a book written jointly with Donald Schon,[2] he developed the concept of single-and double-loop organisational learning. The authors argued that organisational learning involves the detection of errors and their subsequent correction. If this detection and correction allows current policies and objectives to continue, the process is described as single-loop organ-isational learning. If, however, the detection and correction activities modify and change fundamental behaviour, the organisation can be said to have undergone double-loop learning; this necessarily involves learning from others, through discussion and a willingness to accept change. Organisations learn through the agency of indi-viduals, and the appropriate climate must be encouraged to develop the synergy that can be gained through shared experience.

Argyris and Schon's work is a contribution to our perception of learning: they wrote on organisational learning rather than the learn-ing organisation, but in so doing helped to develop the latter concept.

The exposition of the learning organisation that led to a huge interest in the concept came in 1990 in the work of Peter Senge. His important work, *The Fifth Discipline*,[3] has the subtitle *The art and practice of the learning organization*. It is a conceptually difficult work and one that is frequently misunderstood: the fifth discipline of the title does not, for example, refer to organisational learning but to the need for a systems approach.

Senge differentiates learning organisations from traditional authori-tarian 'controlling organisations'. The former are achieved by the mastery of certain disciplines, using the word in a broader sense: to Senge a discipline is a body of practice based in some underlying theory of the world. He argues that five new 'component tech-nologies' or disciplines are gradually converging to innovate learning organisations. The five are:

- *personal mastery* – the capacity to clarify what is most important to the individual
- *team learning* – based on a dialogue in which assumptions are sus-pended so that a genuine thinking together occurs
- *mental models* – the capacity to reflect on internal pictures of the world to see how they shape actions
- *shared vision* – the ability to build a sense of commitment in a group based on what people would really like to create
- *systems thinking* – the capacity for putting things together and seeking holistic solutions.

Systems thinking is the fifth discipline because it is the one that integrates the others, fusing them into a coherent body of theory and practice. In Senge's words: 'It keeps them [the other disciplines] from being separate gimmicks or the latest organisational change fads.'[3] (p12)

Senge's comments on team learning are of considerable value, but his central message is that such activity must not be seen in isolation: it must be underpinned by the fifth discipline. Ironically, therefore, someone who is revered as a guru of the learning organisation should more properly be treated as a major critic of the concept as advocated, since it is frequently viewed in isolation from other corporate activities. In a sense, therefore, the organisation's leadership must buy into the total concept before Senge's learning organisation can be implemented. This makes an important theoretical construct but a demanding idea in practice.

Undoubtedly the concept of the learning organisation has excited many practitioners in the UK. The major criticism, as has been stated, is that it is too imprecise to offer a practical framework for day-to-day activity.

As an illustration, consider the link between individual and organisational learning. It is easy to see that individuals learn – they accumulate knowledge and skills both by design (if they receive training) and absorption. However, in what sense do organisations learn? Certainly the accumulated stock of learning held by individuals is of value to the organisation – this has led to the concept of intellectual and human capital considered in Focus Point 14.

This is an attractive concept, but two questions need to be answered. First, what is organisational learning? Is it more than an addition or summation of individual learning? Second, if it can be identified, how can it be developed? It is easier to answer the second question than the first.

Without doubt a climate or organisational culture can be nurtured where individuals are encouraged to grow by sharing experiences. Where the concept of the learning organisation has disappointed to date, however, is in demonstrating clearly how this can be done.

Focus Point 14: Intellectual and human capital

A simple definition of intellectual capital is:

> The sum of everything the people in the company know that gives
> a competitive advantage in the market.

This definition reflects the early writing of Tom Stewart, a distinguished writer for the US magazine *Fortune*. In 1997 he produced a classic book on the subject.[4] Stewart pioneered the concept of managing intangible corporate assets. A company can be
defined by its intellectual capital rather than its financial capital
(machinery, property and physical resources). Stewart presented
an approach to discovering and defining a company's human
knowledge capital, its information (or structured) capital and consumer capital. In this book he defined intellectual capital as:

> Intellectual material – knowledge, information, intellectual prop-
> erty, experience that can be put to use to create wealth.[4] (px)

The idea that a radical realignment of wealth is under way found
another expression in a 2000 book by Stan Davis and
Christopher Meyer (the joint authors of *Blur*, see pages 12–13).

In *Future Wealth*[5] they argued that everything of value – including
human capital, talent and other intangibles – will be traded in efficient financial markets. Human capital will become the scarcest
resource in business. Competitive advantage will depend on
attracting and keeping the best talent.

Davis and Meyer's challenging book not only considers the implications (for the individual and the organisation) of the development of efficient markets in human capital. It considers the
importance of new approaches to risk and advocates the need for
a new form of social safety nets.

How can individual learning be stretched and leveraged for organisational advantage? One useful volume that explores this area is
Campbell and Luchs' 1997 book *Core Competency-Based Strategy*,[6] but
in general this has proved an elusive idea for the training profession.

Fortunately the emerging discipline of knowledge management can
offer some valuable insights on organisational learning. This will

form the next section. The concept of the learning organisation will be revisited later in this chapter when it will be discussed in a broader context – and one practical approach to the learning organisation will be considered.

Knowledge management

The idea that knowledge can be actively managed to give a competitive advantage is an exciting one. It is another expression of a view that in the modern organisation people are a primary source of competitive advantage. Knowledge management shares a conceptual grounding with intellectual and human capital (and to some extent the learning organisation). It does, however, lend itself to more immediate practical application.

Much of the early stimulus and interest came from the work of Professor Ikujiro Nonaka who, in 1991, wrote an influential article in *Harvard Business Review*, followed two years later by a well-received book.[7,8] Nonaka based his approach on an examination of companies who are 'famous for their ability to respond quickly to customers, create new markets, rapidly develop new products and dominate emergent technologies. The secret of their success is their unique approach to managing the creation of key knowledge.'[7] (pp96–7)

The quotation places the emphasis on the creation of new knowledge; this is logically distinct from managing existing knowledge. To Nonaka new knowledge always starts with the individual; the task is to make that personal knowledge available to others.

In 1999 the (then) Institute of Personnel and Development commissioned Professor Harry Scarbrough of Leicester University Management Centre and Jacky Swan and John Preston of Warwick Business School to undertake a literature review of knowledge management.[9] The report sought to evaluate critically the available literature on both knowledge management and the learning organisation from a human resource perspective: it sought to identify the key features of knowledge management and the learning organisation and their implications for people management.

Investigating the link between the learning organisation and knowledge management was important at the time. The idea of the learning organisation had captured the imagination of many human resource professionals. It did not, however, easily produce visible new activity beyond a general commitment to invest resources in developing people. It was therefore difficult to be certain of any impact – or, indeed, to find things to monitor and measure. Knowledge management, by contrast, did not originate within human resources. Much of the stimulus had come from the wider availability of technology systems that permitted the exchange of information through shared databases. Literature on knowledge management was burgeoning, while literature on the learning organisation seemed to decline. Moreover, the literature review conducted by Scarbrough *et al* appeared to indicate that knowledge management was increasingly viewed as a product of the information systems/information technology industry.

A cynical view could be that the information technology specialist had stolen the human resource professional's clothes. This view is unduly alarmist. What was and remains at issue is a need to provide a coherent approach to build organisational advantage. Scarbrough *et al* mapped knowledge management and the learning organisation in a wide context of managerial theories:

> As our literature review shows, interest in the terminology and ideals of these theories waxes and wanes. If we place them in their context, however, we are better able to understand what they say about the problems confronting firms; we can assess the importance of [knowledge management and the learning organisation] separately from their ability to capture the attention of managers. The inescapable conclusion of such an exercise is that the terms [knowledge management and the learning organisation] will fade away and be replaced by another set of buzzwords and managerial nostrums. However, the demise of these managerial fads will itself be testimony to the phenomena which they seek to address, ie the growing knowledge-intensity of business, the impact of technology on relationships, and the importance of change and innovation. *These factors are not the product of fashion but of history, and in particular of a convergent set of forces which are unleashing fundamental patterns of change on advanced industrial economies.*[9] (p4) [Current author's italics.]

A convergence of interventions

The last sentence of the above quotation is a useful introduction to the next proposition.

Proposition 7

There will be a convergence (or blurring) between knowledge management, performance management and training. All are responses to gaining competitive advantage through people in the information age.

Proposition 7 introduces the term performance management, which was defined in a 1998 book as:

> a strategic and integrated approach to delivering sustained success to organisations by improving the performance of the people who work in them and by developing the capabilities of teams and individual contributors.[10] (p7)

The concept of performance management lies firmly in the domain of human resources (if we don't know something about improving the performance of people, what *do* we know?). Armstrong and Baron – in *Performance Management: The new realities,* from which the above quotation is taken – provide a good overview of the issues. Generally, performance management is about motivating individuals through feedback and targets; it is about providing development opportunities; it is about aligning performance to shared organisational objectives. New tools and mechanisms are emerging to assist that process: most importantly there is a growing interest in multi-source feedback where a range of views on individual performance are sought and fed into the review process.

This convergence, or blurring, outlined in Proposition 7 arises for both practical and conceptual reasons. The case study included at the end of this chapter provides a practical example, based on experience at Ernst & Young. The main purpose was to implement effective multi-source feedback, but a decision to use a familiar technology platform will assist this process of convergence.

‹ The aim should be to create synergies ›

Conceptually, knowledge management, performance management and training seek to maximise the contribution from people. All are interventions. The organisation does something that seeks to improve group or individual performance by extending current capabilities. This involves proactive steps. This is why the term 'training' rather than 'learning' is used. As these activities are extended and aligned, so it will become increasingly hard to delineate and put boundaries between them. Moreover, the aim should be to create synergies. Training interventions should not be seen in isolation. Wherever possible the trainer should seek to identify and draw from models that encourage such a convergence of ideas. In this way areas of overlap and efficiencies in practice will emerge.

Practically, it makes sense if the same technology platform is used. Apart from the argument for building on user familiarity, there are powerful arguments in terms of improved efficiency of process. It is possible, on the intranet, to move between a training module and a database that contains information in a repository. It could be desirable (and is technologically feasible) to embed the latter in the former.

Put simply, from the user's point of view all applications can be accessed on the same personal computer. Questionnaires, guidance and advice arrive through the same route. If what is accessed is a web-based module on (say) the new economic models that are arising from the Internet, it can be described as training. If what is accessed is a commentary or slide pack from the organisation on how the new economic models are affecting the products on offer to customers, it can be described as knowledge management. However, the distinction is immaterial. Similarly, if the user accesses a training module on interpersonal skills it can be described as training intervention. If the user is given, through multi-source feedback, an indication that he or she needs to improve his or her interpersonal skills, it can be described as performance management. If there is a direct link to an interpersonal skills training event (whether a course or a module available on the intranet), it becomes training intervention. Although the blur is not as evident as in the case of training and knowledge management, a blurring of boundaries has taken place.

Encouraging the convergence: two practical views

A blurring between the different processes designed to gain competitive advantage through people is inevitable. Moreover, it should

be encouraged. It will benefit both the organisation and the individuals. As will be seen, it is at the heart of the new paradigm for
training.

The role of the training manager is to assist the organisation to
achieve its objectives by developing the knowledge and skills of the
employees. Connectivity means he or she must work in a different
way. A blurring of knowledge management, performance management and training is just one dimension of the new context in which
he or she will operate. What is important is to construct a conceptual framework in which a strategy can be determined and practical
action can be taken.

The remainder of this chapter will outline such a framework and
present an argument that it should be regarded as a paradigm shift.
First, the work of two commentators, one on knowledge management and one on learning, will be presented. They are chosen
because they are most practical in their analysis.

Nancy Dixon is based at George Washington University. In her
book *Common Knowledge*,[11] she offers a straightforward definition of
knowledge. She also presents an analysis of the use of knowledge in
organisations. Her approach is of value in building a practical framework for knowledge management and in facilitating the convergence
of knowledge management and learning.

Professor Dixon uses the term 'common knowledge' to describe the
knowledge that employees learn from doing the organisation's tasks.
She uses this term to differentiate from book knowledge, regulations,
databases and customer information. Using her description, the
acquisition and spread of common knowledge must be a form of learning. Common knowledge is the 'know-how' rather than the 'know-
what' – and it is the know-how that is unique to a specific company.

> This very specificity is what gives the knowledge gained from
> experience its potential to provide an organization with a competitive
> edge.[11] (p11)

Professor Dixon argues that organisations must reinvent and update
their common knowledge: they achieve this through two different
kinds of knowledge activities.

First, they have to find effective ways to translate their ongoing experience into knowledge – *create* common knowledge. Second, they have to transfer that knowledge across time and space – *leverage* common knowledge.[11] (p17)

These processes do not happen automatically – it takes a certain amount of intention to create knowledge out of experience and to transfer (or leverage) knowledge across time and space. In her book, Professor Dixon identifies five different types of knowledge transfer that can occur in an organisation and suggests ways of facilitating and improving such transfer.

Most importantly, her research showed that one size does not fit all.

> The method that any one organization used to leverage knowledge bore little resemblance to the method that any other organization was using, although each organization seemed to swear by its own process.[11] (p21)

However, although there must be diversity of approach, it is possible to discern what makes a method of knowledge transfer effective in a given situation. Nancy Dixon expressed her findings in terms of three criteria that determine how a transfer will work in a specific situation:

1 Who the intended receiver of the knowledge is in terms of similarity of task and context.
2 The nature of the task in terms of how routine and frequent it is.
3 The type of knowledge that is being transferred.[11] (p22)

The second commentator is Andrew Mayo, who has written extensively on training and learning issues. As a former head of personnel at ICL Europe, he is also conscious of the practical problems surrounding implementation. It is his contribution to the learning organisation literature that is of particular relevance here. In a well-received book, written originally in 1994 with Elizabeth Lank, a colleague at ICL, he defined the learning organisation as follows:

> A Learning Organisation harnesses the full brainpower, knowledge and experience available to it, in order to evolve continually for the benefit of all its stakeholders.[12] (pviii)

‘No organisation today would claim to harness the *full* brainpower available to it’

This definition is, to use the phrase introduced earlier, aspirational. No organisation today would claim to harness the *full* brainpower available to it. What managers (and especially those who carry responsibility for training) can do is to put processes in place to achieve this aim. Where Andrew Mayo's analysis is of value is that his approach to the learning organisation emphasises the need for a variety of such processes to be put in place on a consistent basis. His model is presented in diagrammatic form as Figure 6.

In his book, Mayo helpfully introduces a checklist questionnaire that outlines the steps and issues that must be considered to implement the model. This list embraces the gamut of practical issues that need to be discussed to advance towards the aspirational goal of his definition of the learning organisation.

The identification of the appropriate practical steps that should be taken to develop competitive advantage through people lies at the heart of the training function. If they are undertaken in a co-ordinated manner, they could sensibly be defined as promoting organisational learning. There has been much debate (often insuffi-

Figure 6
THE COMPLETE LEARNING ORGANISATION

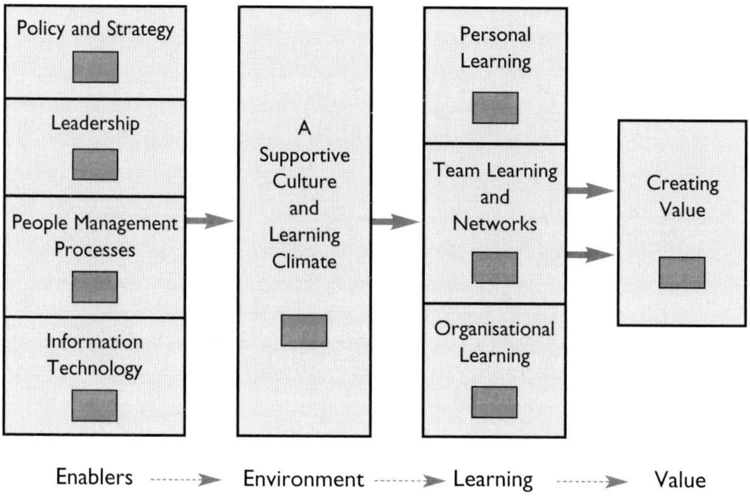

(Reproduced with permission from *The Power of Learning*[12])

ciently rigorous) in the training profession on organisational learning and the learning organisation. This could sensibly evaporate and the focus move to a discussion on the practical steps needed to encourage the individual to acquire know-how and to share/leverage it in the organisation.

The learning organisation revisited

The preceding analysis of the convergence of process and the outline of Nancy Dixon's and Andrew Mayo's refreshingly practical approaches to implementation helpfully introduce the next proposition.

Proposition 8

E-learning can give new meaning to the concept of the learning organisation.

The underlying suggestion behind this proposition is deceptively simple. Efforts to create a learning organisation are characterised by co-ordinated activities that attempt to foster individual learning. Although this is conceptually straightforward, such activities are demanding in practice. E-learning alters the scope of these activities and makes co-ordination easier to understand.

A starting point is to return to one of the key themes introduced earlier in this chapter: the value of the distinction between learning and training. To reiterate: the former lies in the domain of the individual; the latter in the domain of the organisation.

In the connected economy, information, guidance and support can be delivered electronically. This has many advantages and, as has been recognised, some limitations. If it is appropriately structured, organised and supported it is a powerful enabler for individual learning – this is a definition of effective e-learning.

A learning organisation, then, would be one where the thrust of the organisational training intervention is focused on implementing effective e-learning in the wider cultural context. It would be characterised by the following:

✍ Efforts have been made to inculcate learning in all activities.

✍ It is accepted in the culture that learning should take place beyond what is narrowly defined as essential.

✍ Training interventions have, as a matter of course, been designed to encourage the learner to take responsibility and ownership for learning.

The above is more properly viewed as a description of the activities involved in creating a learning organisation than as a definition of a learning organisation. It sees the learning organisation as an aspirational rather than an absolute concept. It avoids unhelpful debates about whether an organisation is or is not a learning organisation. It avoids the imprecision of definition that have so often characterised discussions of the learning organisation concept.

It also recognises that many individuals themselves will need to make a personal paradigm shift. They will need to recognise that their acceptance of responsibility for their own development is the key to employability. Those charged with increasing the human capital of the organisation will need to acquire the skills to help the learner make this attitudinal shift.

Irrespective of the future of the concept of the learning organisation, the next proposition can be offered with confidence.

Proposition 9

A new paradigm based on learner-centred interventions will emerge. This will draw on business, learning and traditional training models.

What Proposition 9 is saying is that in a relatively short time (perhaps two or three years), those involved in training in organisations will have developed a new way of looking at their world. They will share a new conceptual framework in which to construct models and determine practice.

Connectivity will create a convergence between the different approaches available to gain competitive advantage through people.

Together with other technology enablers, it will allow the focus to be placed on the individual learner. It is always dangerous to predict the future – and the impact of the Internet makes it an even more hazardous process. Often in human resource development models are regarded as absolute when they should be viewed as evolving. We need to be comfortable with uncertainty and a more tentative approach. However, the new paradigm will be characterised by:

- emphasis on the learner and his or her acceptance of responsibility
- a holistic (or integrated) approach to creating competitive advantage through people in the organisation
- the need to ensure that resources are focused appropriately and managed effectively.

The phrase 'learner-centred interventions' is offered as a label for this paradigm – with trepidation!

References

1   PISKURICH G. M. *and* SANDERS E. S. *ASTD Models for Learning Technologies: Roles, competencies and outputs.* Alexandria, Va., ASTD, 1998.

2   ARGYRIS C. *and* SCHON D. A. *Organizational Learning: A theory of action perspective.* Wokingham, Addison-Wesley, 1978.

3   SENGE P. M. *The Fifth Discipline: The art and practice of the learning organization.* New York, Doubleday, 1990.

4   STEWART T. A. *Intellectual Capital.* London, Nicholas Brealey Publishing, 1997.

5   DAVIS S. *and* MEYER C. *Future Wealth.* Boston, Mass., Ernst & Young Centre for Business Innovation/Harvard Business School Press, 2000.

6   CAMPBELL A. *and* LUCHS K. S. (EDS) *Core Competency-Based Strategy.* London, International Thomson Business Press, 1997.

7   NONAKA I. 'The knowledge-creating company'. *Harvard Business Review.* Vol. 69, No. 6, 1991, pp96–104.

8   NONAKA I. *and* TAAKKEUCHI H. *The Knowledge-Creating Company: How Japanese companies create the dynamics of innovation.* Oxford, Oxford University Press, 1993.

9   SCARBROUGH H., SWAN J. *and* PRESTON J. *Knowledge*

Management: A literature review. London, Institute of Personnel and Development, 1999.

10   ARMSTRONG M. *and* BARON A. *Performance Management: The new realities.* London, Institute of Personnel and Development, 1998.

11   DIXON N. M. *Common Knowledge.* Boston, Mass, Harvard Business School Press, 2000.

12   MAYO A. *and* LANK E. *The Power of Learning: A guide to gaining competitive advantage.* London, Institute of Personnel and Development, 1994.

Case Study

PERFORMANCE FEEDBACK AT ERNST & YOUNG

Ernst & Young is a leading business advisory firm employing some 7,000 people in the UK, the majority of whom work in the assurance and tax disciplines.

There is a strong commitment to develop talent ('growing our people') and an acceptance of the importance of feedback. Such feedback is regarded as valuable both for short-term performance issues and for long-term skills acquisition, with a consequent link to personal growth. Although the process used is known as 360-degree feedback, it is technically more properly described as multi-source feedback. Views on an individual's performance and development needs are sought from the individual's manager, subordinates and peers.

In the mid-1990s, formalised 360-degree feedback was used for the annual appraisal review of some 400 Ernst & Young partners. Respondents were asked to assess partner performance against 40 separate indicators – using a rating system. The process was paper-based: completed forms were sent back to an administrator who collated results while maintaining confidentiality.

The results formed an input to an annual performance discussion between the partner and a more senior member of the Ernst &

Young Partnership. A paper-based system was also used, at a lower level in the organisation, to provide input to a development workshop for managers.

It was recognised that there was a need to automate the process, and in 1998 an external consulting organisation was commissioned to provide a bureau service. Although this produced the desired end result, there were evident problems. The person under review felt impotent and not in control of the process. Time lags were inevitable and there was insufficient flexibility in a process that was driven by a third party.

In the following year, a decision was made to move to a process using Lotus Notes – the technology platform that is used throughout Ernst & Young in the UK. The vision was to create a fully automated, paperless system driven by the individual. This would allow the cost-effective production of reports that would be available as soon as the respondents had completed their feedback. Eventually, it could be accessed through the Ernst & Young intranet, but Lotus Notes was chosen as the original platform because it had a high degree of user familiarity.

After a tender process, an external consultancy, the Performance Management Group, was contracted to design and deliver the system. All those reviewed in the process were required to nominate a minimum of five individuals. These five, and the individual under review, were asked to rate performance against competency indicators and to add a sentence or two of narrative for each competency. These comments would not be attributed to any specific author, but would be collated as a report for the individual and his or her boss at performance review time.

Timescale was tight for the first year. There was a need to customise the consultant's existing Lotus Notes-based product. Against tight deadlines, the system, called ORBIT 360°, was made available for partners and senior managers in time for the review round, and subsequently extended lower down the organisation.

According to Julie Holden, Director of Internal Consulting, who was responsible for implementation, the achievement of this timescale reflected considerations beyond technological implementation. There was a base level of maturity and acceptance of the value of feedback throughout the organisation. Senior staff did not need to buy into the principle and already recognised the value of providing and receiving feedback. Paper-based systems caused them frustration.

The next step will be to extend links between a number of tools and processes delivered through the Lotus Notes platform. They must be more closely aligned in content, and access between the systems must be made easier. Performance management systems will, for example, change as global systems are made available – partner performance measures will be standardised across the world. A new learning portal, 'Look Here for Learning', has been introduced and the links between performance management, 'Look Here for Learning' and Ernst & Young's knowledge management system need to be better signposted.

This case study example is particularly appropriate to the argument of the chapter because of the deliberate use of a familiar groupware (in this case Lotus Notes). Groupware can be defined as a technology platform that supports communications, collaboration and co-ordination between individuals in an organisation. The choice of the groupware reflected its functionality, acceptability and the desire to avoid the introduction of an entirely new platform. Convergence between knowledge, performance management and learning has been enhanced as a result.

My thanks to my colleague, Julie Holden, for her assistance in the preparation of this case study.

Chapter 4

Developing the agenda for the organisation

Our similarities are different

Some general principles

The impact of the connected economy on training extends over all aspects of training activity. The last chapter concluded with the argument that a new paradigm for training will emerge: this was described as learner-centred interventions. It will draw on business, learning and traditional training models. The challenge is to use the new opportunity presented by connectivity to put the focus on the learners and to define training interventions so as to assist and facilitate their relevant learning. In facing this challenge, all those responsible for training must draw on insights and information from a variety of sources – especially the new business models that have emerged from the arrival of the Internet.

‹ The challenge is to put the focus on the learners ›

To revisit the arguments advanced so far, the connected economy has led to new opportunities in all facets of economic and commercial activity through enhanced communications. More generally, the nature of market competition and the emergence of new business models mean different skills will be required in most organisations. The training sector will be affected as much as other industries. A powerful new platform has emerged: a proportion of training will be delivered through the Internet/intranet using web-based protocols. The new platform of connectivity will provide a new opportunity for effective training that goes far beyond training design and delivery.

In this chapter the focus will be on the action needed at the micro-level. All those charged with the implementation of training are facing tough choices. What should they do in their organisation – starting next Monday morning? How should they meet the challenge posed by this disruptive technology? How, most importantly, can expensive mistakes be avoided?

Although every organisation faces different circumstances, some general principles are emerging. These follow from the application of the new Internet business models to the training situation. One list, which draws from the work of Stan Davis and Chris Meyer, is set out in Focus Point 15. The argument, which must be stressed, is that everyone should should look at their organisation and see what is appropriate. At the same time they should constantly scan the external environment to seek to identify the opportunities that technology can offer. So far these opportunities (or best practice) have been realised in the commercial/economic arena, rather than in training.

Focus Point 15: Some general principles for implementing e-learning

The principles set out below were adapted from a consideration of '50 ways to blur your business', contained in Stan Davis and Chris Meyer's *Blur* (see reference 11, Chapter 1).

- *Try to connect everything with everything* – seek information flows with all parties that are involved in the design, delivery and use of training, whether inside or outside your organisation.
- *Use different outlets for delivery* – the end user (the learner) will benefit from choice of access.
- *Deliver anytime anywhere and communicate and take feedback online* – give the learners easy access and the power to decide when to learn, and allow them to send back their views
- *Customise your offer for the user and improve it continuously* – tailor your offer to each individual user – let them have it their way.

With acknowledgement and thanks to Stan Davis and Chris Meyer.

At the end of this chapter a number of case studies are presented. These concern organisations that have drawn up (or are in the process of drawing up) an appropriate agenda for the introduction of e-learning. Those responsible have found it necessary to make what may be called robust decisions. These may be described as short-term decisions that carry the organisation forward to an agreed objective, but do not prevent the opportunity of proceeding differently if circumstances change (the expression was originally defined by Robert Eccles of Harvard Business School). The pace of recent change, and the fact that the technological platforms available to the trainer are 'borrowed' from other uses in the organisation, have made life difficult for the training manager. Robust decisions are definitely required.

As will be seen, the subjects of the case studies have used different approaches and are at different stages in their development. Their training managers are facing very different situations. CERN, Hanover Housing Association, Clifford Chance and the Post Office differ in terms of size, objectives, history and cultures. Some of their human resource professionals have adopted a bold and adventurous implementation plan that may carry a degree of risk; others have been tentative and measured. All, however, have paid regard to the proposition set out below.

Proposition 10

Training managers should identify the appropriate wins in their organisation rather than letting the availability of technology determine their agenda.

The key word here is *appropriate*: in an earlier draft the phrase 'easy wins' was used. The appropriate wins may indeed be the easy wins – the initiatives that can be delivered through the existing technology platforms and demonstrate quickly what e-learning is about. An introduction of a learning portal would be a good example. However, the appropriate choice could be something that is seen to bring real value to the organisation in achieving its wider objectives. Giving an internal subject-matter expert the capability to author web-based training could be an example of an entirely appropriate win which

may be far from easy. This compromise between easy (and by implication quick and cheap) and high-value (by implication expensive
and demanding) seems to run as an undercurrent in the thoughts of
the training managers interviewed in the course of the case studies.

Costing and budgeting

One of the most critical questions affecting the ability to make
robust decisions is the need for a cost estimate. Given the speed of
change, it would be misleading to offer any hard and fast guidance:
remember, Moore's law (see page 2) states that every 18 months
computer processing power doubles while cost holds constant.

Any 'at the time of writing' estimates will be out of date by the time
of reading. Some figures were helpfully offered in some of the case
studies, but these reflected the particular approach used by that
organisation at that time.

An exercise based on the relative costs of installing one of the then
available learning systems was undertaken by Ernst & Young in
1999. This indicated that if this option was chosen, two elements
were involved: first, the initial installation costs (which must obviously depend on the stake of the host organisation's IT platforms),
and second, an ongoing charge thereafter. This ongoing charge
would cover the licence of the system and payment for content. For
what it is worth, the figures at that time suggested set-up costs
ranging between £10,000 and £60,000 (though one system could
cost £250,000!) and ongoing access costs between £5 and £10 per
user per year.

Another approach to cost estimation is to assume that up to a quarter of the training volume will be delivered using technology.
Training delivered through this means will be cheaper: this is often
seen as the main justification. A rough estimate of ongoing costs per
user at, say, 10 per cent of training budget could be set for the initial
forays into the e-learning arena – if a piecemeal rather than a big
bang approach is to be adopted.

One point to emerge from this hypothetical discussion is that the
nature of the investment decision has changed. The traditional resourc-

ing decision facing the training manager was straightforward: a course was costed; budgets were set on the basis of the cost of the courses offered on the training menu. Depending on the organisation, the costs could be charged back to individual users or their departments. Budget pressure would lead to courses being withdrawn from the menu.

In e-learning, a different sort of investment decision is required. It is a project decision: an initial investment is required that will lead to ongoing savings in future years. Fortunately there is considerable experience in the IT departments of such project costing – it is to them that the training manager must look for guidance and advice.

Single frames

Single frames can assist in the process of making robust decisions. To recapitulate: a single frame is a diagram on one page that captures key concepts in a graphical form. A major advantage of single frames is that they can form the basis of a useful exchange and dialogue. This occurs when they are completed in conjunction with another party – summary phrases are inserted in the empty boxes as an outcome of a focused meeting. Ernst & Young has developed the single frame as an approach to client relationships. Exactly the same principle applies to relationships with internal clients. A number of single frames will now be presented. In each case it is recommended that the training manager seeks advice inside and outside the organisation and completes the relevant text.

The first two single frames are reproduced as Figures 7 and 8: they are an e-learning transformation matrix and an instrument for defining the e-learning solution that is appropriate to the organisation. They are offered to the reader to use as he or she wishes, but with a firm recommendation that other stakeholders in the organisation should be involved. To repeat: single frames can form the basis of a useful exchange and dialogue.

Figure 7 simply recasts the Ernst & Young transformation matrix introduced in Chapter 1 (see Figure 1, page 16, and the accompanying text, pages 14–18). The reader is recommended to refer back to this section. The argument was that specific initiatives were needed to transform organisations to become an e-business and that four stages in this transformation could be identified. Figure 7 seeks to

Figure 7
E-LEARNING TRANSFORMATION FRAMEWORK

	Transformation →			
	E-Information (accessing and delivering information through an electronic channel)	E-Exchange (formal and quantified entry and exchange of learning opportunities)	E-Delivery (identification and delivery of services using an intranet)	E-Training (connections with all aspects of corporate development strategies; permeable boundaries with external learning opportunities)
Needs identification				
Sources of training solutions				
Delivery of training				
Management of resources				

Figure 8
DEFINING THE E-LEARNING SOLUTION

New business model for the organisation (how will the organisation compete in the connected economy?)	

Marketplace (how do users gain information on learning opportunities?)	
Customer connections (how does the market clear?)	
Supply chain (how is design and delivery organised?)	

express this transformation in training or learning terms. The column headings describe the stages of the transformation. The headings along the rows identify four key activities undertaken by those responsible for training.

Figure 8 'Defining the e-learning solution' reflects some of the principles set out in Focus Point 15. It reinforces the argument that training is a market just like any other: the question 'how does the market clear?', for example, asks the training manager to consider how learning resources are actually allocated to the learner. Does a price mechanism operate (by charging for courses against departmental budgets, for example), or is supply and demand applied in another way (by compulsory training, for example)?

‹In all transmissions to the learner a value chain is involved›

Figure 8 also reintroduces the term *supply chain*. This was defined in Chapter 1 (pages 11–12) as 'a system whose constituent parts include material suppliers, production facilities, distribution services and customers linked together via the forward flow of materials and the forward and backward flow of information'. When the term was introduced it was argued that the Internet would have a significant effect on the value or supply chain. Although the expression *supply chain* is more common (supply chain management is a well-explored and well-recognised process), in many ways the phrase *value chain* is preferable. Training managers do not instinctively think in terms of the value chain, but in all transmissions to the learner (the end consumer) a value chain is involved. Given the increasing blur caused by the Internet, the phrase *value web* (rather than value chain) is starting to be used. This emphasises the importance of different contributions and varying relationships at all stages of transmission.

An outline value chain is shown in diagrammatic form as Figure 9. It is important for those responsible for training to consider the chain that applies in their organisation. The Internet will, with certainty, affect that value chain and offer new opportunities. There are often significant transaction costs between each of the components of the value chain, and the Internet (through the market effect, see Focus Point 5, page 7) will force greater efficiency. This is summarised in the next proposition.

Figure 9
THE SUPPLY OR VALUE CHAIN

A generic model

How it might appear to the training manager

What is the training content – the building blocks of knowledge and skill elements? Who creates or supplies them?	How are the building blocks put together into a cohesive module or programme? Is this done in-house or outsourced?	How are the modules or programmes delivered? Are they courses, technology-based training or experiential events?	How are the end users made aware of the events? How do they access them?	What support does the end user (the learner) need and how is it delivered? What is the reinforcement of learning (the after-sales service)

Raw Materials → Manufacturing → Distribution → Marketing → Customer

Proposition 11

Training professionals should investigate the new business models. They should review their value chains.

The e-learning agenda

The next single frame, Figure 10, is a general tool that could be applied in a whole host of situations and in organisations that were at very different stages in their thinking. The tool should be of interest to all responsible for developing human resources, but of particular value to the training manager.

The top half of this single frame offers a training manager an opportunity to map the current and desired future states and to identify the major enablers and blockages.

First, the left-hand box (current state) suggests that a simple SWOT (strengths, weaknesses, opportunities, threats) analysis should be conducted – preferably in conjunction with other people outside the training department.

Figure 10
DETERMINING YOUR E-TRAINING AGENDA

Current State	Future State	Key Issues

Strengths	Weaknesses	Training and the business	State of technology
			Intranet/extranet
			Training delivery to date
Opportunities	Threats	Structure and role of the training department	Learning support
			Coaching capability
			Awareness of training suppliers

E-Training Options

Protect the core	Change the game
Current Initiatives Future Initiatives	Current Initiatives Future Initiatives

The middle box looks at the future state. What is the preferred relationship between training and the business? How can training as a whole add value? Given this relationship, how should the training department be structured and how should its role be defined?

The third box contains a list of key issues that need to be considered at the beginning of the transition to e-learning.

The first two (the state of technology and intranet/extranet) demand a discussion with those responsible for information technology in the organisation. It is a self-evident proposition that any e-training initiative:

✍ should not put an unacceptable load on the network and services
✍ should be consistent and compatible with other developments.

The next key issues (training delivery to date, learning support, coaching capability and awareness of training suppliers) invite a consideration of the current pattern of delivery and the opportunity for change. As will be argued in the next chapter, the introduction of e-learning will focus attention on some of the softer aspects of training. The concept of learning support will be developed more fully later (see Chapter 5) and coaching will be a key element in that provision.

The bottom half of Figure 10 invites decisions. The options can be divided into two. One option is to protect the core: the strategy here is to do enough to maintain the position of training in the organisation. What steps or initiatives need to be taken now and in the future to ensure that training does not become marginalised (or even abolished!)? This may sound defensive, but for some the threat may be real. When technology-based training was in its early stages, an over-reliance on computer-based training undoubtedly led to a failure to recognise some positive aspects of face-to-face training. For some organisations and individuals, the consequence would have been dire.

The alternative strategy is labelled 'Change the game'. At its boldest this means that the training manager will seek a rapid transformation based on e-learning. He or she will seek different relationships in the organisation, based on different methods of delivery and earn new respect. Leading-edge status in the profession may beckon! Such a course, while it may only be for the bold, should always be considered and its consequences assessed. If not, some easy short-term gains could be overlooked.

Is technology necessarily the best course?

So far the frameworks and approaches outlined in this chapter have assumed a general acceptance of the value of e-learning: that it is beneficial and indeed that its advance is inevitable.

‹But you can't replace the classroom experience›

To many decision-makers in organisations the proposition is far from self-evident. Such sentiments will be shared by those in the training community who have not had exposure to the potential of

Internet/intranet-based approaches. The objection is often expressed as 'But you can't replace the classroom experience.'

This objection should not be dismissed lightly. It has much substance. It was also given much credence by experience with previous generations of computer-based training (see Chapter 2, Focus Point 11, page 36). The improved delivery offered by the CD-ROM was often pushed beyond its sensible limits and some restricted soft skills training (even extending to assertiveness skills) was offered as a substitute to course-based personal interaction. This problem continues as web-based training is oversold by organisations and individuals who do not always demonstrate an appreciation of the principles underlying effective learning.

For most people who have explored the opportunities created by the new technology platforms, the argument has moved beyond this stage. The potential of e-learning is enormous, but it must be introduced in an appropriate structure. The following proposition therefore would command general support.

Proposition 12

E-learning will be most effective for the acquisition of knowledge and least effective where interpersonal interaction is needed for learning.

Here it is worth remembering that the American Society for Training and Development survey outlined in Chapter 2 (page 39) quoted a figure of 22 per cent for training delivered through the intranet. By general recognition, Motorola is considered one of the most sophisticated organisations in terms of its approach to e-learning. Its experience will form the basis of a case study to be considered in the next chapter. Motorola's target for training delivered through alternative (non-classroom) means was 30 per cent for 2000, rising to 50 per cent by 2003.

Even on the most bullish of estimates, there will continue to be a high proportion of training delivered by non-technological means. There will continue to be a balance between different approaches.

What is important is that this balance is considered and planned appropriately. This will be examined further in the next chapter, where 'bias for the classroom' will be discussed as an issue.

Irrespective of the sophistication of the organisation, e-learning should never be introduced in isolation, as the next proposition suggests.

Proposition 13

E-learning will be most effective as part of a systematic approach involving classroom and experiential learning with appropriate support.

Much of the discussion to support this proposition falls in the next chapter, where issues of learner support are considered. The phrase 'experiential learning' needs some explanation: it refers to the activities that support an individual's ongoing development. Mentoring, coaching, action learning and self-managed learning (see pages 152–157) are all examples. Here the individual learns through experience, but the organisation intervenes to create or support that experience.

IBM offers a good example of the way that a systematic approach involving this balance can be developed. It forms the last of the case studies that follow at the end of this chapter. IBM, however, is a very sophisticated organisation. Few training managers have the time or resources to develop their own all-embracing model. What this chapter has sought to do is to assist them with two things. First, it has sought to demystify e-learning. Progress is not about buying a learning system; it is about identifying the appropriate solution for the organisation and making robust decisions. Second, it has offered a series of instruments (known as single frames) that provide a framework for discussion in the reader's own organisation. Ultimately he or she must carry the responsibility of progressing the debate. Finally it illustrates, through the case studies that follow, the diverse approaches that are being adopted by thoughtful human resource professionals. My thanks to them for their willingness to share their experience with others.

Case Study

CERN

Background

CERN is the European Organization for Nuclear Research (otherwise known as the European Laboratory for Particle Physics), established in 1953 to:

> provide for collaboration among European States in nuclear research of a pure scientific and fundamental character and in research essentially related thereto. The organization shall have no concern with work for military requirements and the results of its experimental and practical work shall be published.

CERN (an independent international organisation pre-dating the European Union) provides its member states with the facilities to carry out research into the basic structure of matter and the fundamental laws of nature via high-energy particle accelerators and detectors. The UK was a founding member of CERN and remains very actively involved through many university physics departments, the Rutherford Appleton Laboratory (RAL) and the Particle Physics and Astronomy Research Council (PPARC).

Over the subsequent half-century the fundamental objectives – collaboration amongst scientists in leading-edge particle physics – remain unchanged. However, this collaboration has extended beyond Europe to the rest of the world (http://public.web.cern.ch/Public/Welcome.html). CERN is now the leading world laboratory in this field, with active participation from countries such as the USA, Japan, Russia, China and India, as well as its member states.

Most interestingly from the point of view of this book, the World Wide Web was born at CERN as a vehicle to allow the data for scientific research to be shared across boundaries (see page 2 and 4).

CERN now embraces a network of some 10,000 people. The headquarters is at a large site in Geneva where approximately 2,700 people are employed, with another 600 on short-term assignments. CERN employs very few research physicists directly, since the research is conducted primarily by physicists in universities and national institutes throughout Europe, and indeed the world. CERN employees are engineers, applied physicists, computer specialists and technicians, plus administrative support staff. Evidently, and this has been shaped by CERN's approach to learning and development, they are mainly knowledge workers who are generally confident with technology and its uses. In addition, there are 6,000 people who share their time between their home university and CERN, and a further 1,000 people who perform some outsourced activities on the CERN site.

All 10,000 are eligible to access and take advantage of CERN's training provision.

CERN was a comparatively early entrant into e-learning. Two developments – web-based training and a current research and education initiative – are of particular interest.

Web-based training
CERN has invested in training that is delivered to the desktop via the Web. This approach aims to provide:

- just-in-time training for people who are not able to wait for an instructor-led course
- pre-course support for people who wish to start learning a subject before they start an instructor-led course
- post-course reference material for people who need to review topics they have learned on an instructor-led course
- structured learning material for people who do not have time to follow an instructor-led course
- learning material presented in easy-to-review modules for people who want to decide if they need to follow an instructor-led course.

For a small cost (far less than the cost of access to CERN's course-based training), participants can get unlimited access to a full set of courses from the suppliers NETg and Ziff Davis.

The original pilot of web-based training took place in 1998 and more testing followed in 1999 before a decision to commit was made. A dedicated NETg server has been installed, while access to Ziff Davis packages are gained through the supplier's own server in the USA. The second solution provides the added value of giving immediate access to new course offerings as they are published and avoids maintenance overheads.

CERN is confident that this approach has resulted in value for both the organisation and the individual, but would offer two words of caution. First, resources have not permitted it to give the marketing support it feels the initiative deserves: 'These things don't fly by themselves.' It would also like to have more time to devote to an analysis of the usage statistics generated by the two systems. This would lead to a more fundamental evaluation of impact.

It has, however, more than enough information to convince it that this is an appropriate form of training for the right person. In the words of Mick Storr, CERN's head of technical training:

> Training delivered to the desktop via the Web is attractive for certain types of people. It appeals to: those with an academic bent, people who have been through university, people who are used to learning and used to teaching themselves. For people for whom the computer is an obstacle, this approach is bound to be less useful.

Web-based training has not resulted in the elimination of course-based training but fills an important gap for an extended community. It is likely to become increasingly important in the training of new staff members and will complement course-based training. As Bill Blair, head of the training and development group, puts it:

> It releases time and resources to allow us to produce better instructor-led programmes.

Accessing seminar resource information
CERN's technical e-learning project initially concentrated on access to content obtained through two suppliers. The Ziff Davis content allows participants to join chat rooms and instructor-led virtual training, but such excursions by CERN participants have been limited. CERN has not sought to author or customise con-

tent. Instead it has developed a second and complementary strand of e-learning designed to exploit and promote its rich in-house academic and technical seminar programmes.

CERN is currently collaborating with the University of Michigan in a venture designed to capture and catalogue seminars for play-back via the Web, including full video, audio and visual support material using minimal (less than 56 kbaud) bandwidth require-ment. This means that these seminars will be accessible to anyone worldwide with a typical home modem using standard web browsers and free publicly available video playback soft-ware. A significant number of recordings have already been made and can be viewed, along with details of the project (http://webcast.cern.ch/Projects/WebLectureArchive/index.html).

The project is now being extended to investigate the potential of asynchronous (see page 115) virtual classrooms. The barriers surrounding intellectual property will have to be resolved before these techniques can be exploited for dissemination of commer-cial course offerings.

Overview

CERN is unusually well placed to introduce web-based training. Organisationally it shares knowledge between staff who are com-puter-literate and are likely to be self-motivated. The CERN human resource and training professionals see many possibilities for extension – even with the existing technology infrastructure. They are, however, at pains to emphasise the need for more resource support *if* maximum leverage and value is to be gained. In the words of Bill Blair:

> Web-based training is an exciting addition to the menu of train-ing methods. For some people with the appropriately disciplined mindset it could fulfill almost all their training needs. However, the temptation to suppress other forms of training and give staff unassisted access to a vast library of web-based courses should be avoided. Key factors in the successful use of web-based courses are:
>
> **Complementarity** – web-based training is best used as a com-plement to other forms of training

Effectiveness – there should be prior assessment of the suitability of the web-based course(s) for the organisation and for the individual, and then ongoing evaluation of the progress achieved by individuals using web-based learning

Resources – adequate resources should be allocated both for the initial assessment and then for marketing and support for the web-based training operation

'Nous' – flair and knowledge of the culture of the organisation help a lot in identifying training needs and appropriate web-based courses to meet these needs, and above all, in delivering results.

Full information on CERN's training programmes is available on http://public.web.cern.ch/Public/TRAINING/eduintro.html.

My thanks to Bill Blair and Mick Storr for their assistance in the preparation of this case study.

Case Study

HANOVER HOUSING ASSOCIATION

Background
Hanover Housing Association exists to provide sheltered accommodation for older or disabled people. It is a non-profit-making organisation, with elements of a charitable trust. In 1999 turnover was just over £30 million. The head office is in Staines, Middlesex, and there are four regional offices in the North, Midlands, South-East and South-West (www.hanover.org.uk).

The regions are responsible for housing management and services to residents on some 450 estates. The estates can range from a few units to over 200 houses; geographically they extend from Cumbria to Cornwall. There are also a number of owner-occupied houses where elderly owners draw on Hanover's services.

Hanover employ some 750 staff. About half of these staff are involved in managing the housing stock in the Regions. There is a hierarchy of roles. Hanover has a strong commitment to IT and all estate managers (who carry responsibility for day-to-day housing matters) have a stand-alone PC with access to the company's intranet. The other half of the staff undertake a variety of activities designed to support the central objective of provision of accommodation for the elderly and disabled.

The focus of training

In January 2000 Hanover appointed a new training manager – Bobby Davis. She inherited a situation where there had been a number of ad hoc interventions, at national and regional level, to provide skills training delivered through a variety of external suppliers. Bobby Davis took an early decision to introduce a consistent and coherent pattern of training across Hanover using appropriate technology enablers. This decision reflected her previous experience: before joining Hanover she had been a captain in the Royal Corps of Signals and had developed and implemented a computer-based training (CBT) programme for skills and trade training for soldiers involved in the provision of communications.

This proved a successful intervention in the Army and led her to regard technology-based training in a positive light, provided it is part of a co-ordinated programme, including instructor-led training. It can be both more effective (in terms of learning) and more efficient (in terms of resources). In her words:

> Technology-based training is particularly good for consolidating learning. IT access allows you to check content in advance of a workshop; the staff are aware of the key elements of vocabulary when they attend and their participation is enhanced; they can consolidate and review more effectively after the event.

> This is not to denigrate the workshop as a method of learning. Participants benefit from interaction – particularly in an organisation like Hanover, which has a wide geographical spread. The aim is to make the classroom element concentrated so travelling costs are minimised.

An early decision was made to build a solution exploring the existing IT infrastructure and, most importantly, to produce internal content rather than buy generic material:

Hanover is a very particular organisation and needs a particular form of training. Previously, when staff went on an external course they had difficulty relating it to the challenges encountered in the workplace.

The chosen approach

After an initial discussion with Hanover's internal IT services team, a decision was taken to commission a software company, Fourth Broadcast Network (4BN), to design delivery platforms and assist in the presentation of content. The aim was to design, develop and deliver a series of modules, relevant to Hanover, that could be accessed by staff over their PCs. Modules, which would be designed by the training manager, would consist of PowerPoint presentations, video extracts and purchased CD-ROMs. All would be badged with Hanover's house style.

Early explorations involving Hanover Training, its IT department and the software company identified a practical problem on delivery. If the intended modules with their video clips and other elements were to be distributed via Hanover's company intranet, the whole system could slow down disastrously. A decision therefore was taken to use an alternative delivery platform: 10 stand-alone PCs would be placed in convenient geographically dispersed locations and dedicated to the training modules; the content would be placed on back-up servers at each of the locations.

Three training programmes have been prepared and will be piloted on chosen populations. One of the modules is shown as Figure 11. This is intended to offer information about Hanover to all new staff as their induction process.

A second early module concerns the policy and procedures for use across the organisation. A third is much more ambitious. This involves the delivery of a limited set of management training modules and is illustrated as Figure 12. As can be seen, each element may be regarded as a stand-alone module, is centred on a one-day workshop and makes considerable use of existing generic training material. All of these modules are linked to the Association's competency framework. Other modules are

Figure 11

HANOVER HOUSING ASSOCIATION INDUCTION MODULE

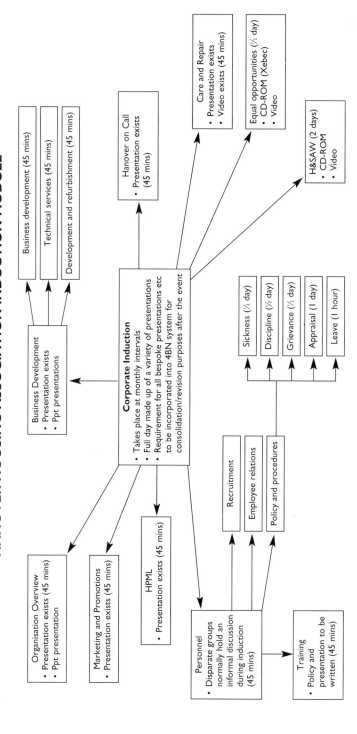

planned and many of these reflect Hanover's approach to housing management. The big gains are thought to arise from company-specific activities.

An indicative cost estimate is for an initial outlay of £25,000. Each module or element will then cost between £1,500 and £4,000. In the first financial year a total of approximately £30,000 has been set aside for the transition to technology-based training.

Learner access

Hanover has been bold and decisive. It has clear business reasons and can justify an approach based on building and distributing customised modules. The challenge facing it is the acceptability of this approach to the end user. Bluntly, will the training material be used, and by the right people? While this challenge has not been addressed, it has, however, been recognised.

Bobby Davis argues that she starts with several advantages. There is a very strong commitment from the senior management. Monthly progress reports have been requested by the corporate management team. The Association makes good use of IT and most staff are comfortable with this approach to communication and dissemination of information. Usage statistics will allow monitoring of areas where take-up proves low. A contingency is to place some material on CD-ROMs for those people who do not have easy access to the designated training PCs in the regional offices.

Bobby recognises, however, that maintaining access and use across the organisation is a major challenge:

> Because they are not in all the main office, there is a danger that remote staff will not make much use of the material. We will need to encourage them to access the training PC whenever they go to the sites. At the end of the day, it is a matter of monitoring, marketing and plugging away.

My thanks to Bobby Davis for her assistance in the preparation of this case study.

Figure 12
HANOVER HOUSING ASSOCIATION MANAGEMENT TRAINING

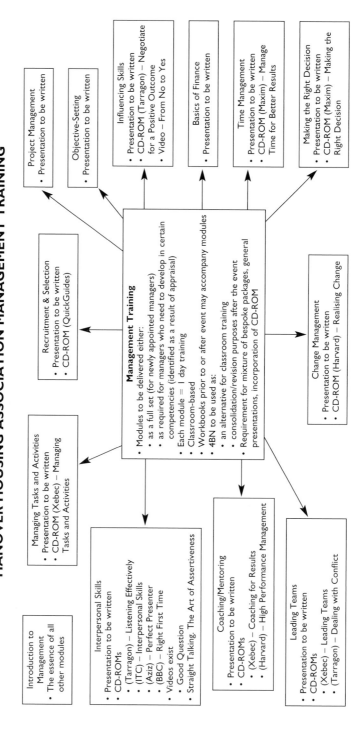

Management Training
- Modules to be delivered either:
  - as a full set (for newly appointed managers)
  - as required for managers who need to develop in certain competencies (identified as a result of appraisal)
- Each module = 1 day training
- Classroom-based
- Workbooks prior to or after event may accompany modules
- 4BN to be used as:
  - an alternative for classroom training
  - consolidation/revision purposes after the event
- Requirement for mixture of bespoke packages, general presentations, incorporation of CD-ROM

Introduction to Management
- The essence of all other modules

Managing Tasks and Activities
- Presentation to be written
- CD-ROM (Xebec) – Managing Tasks and Activities

Recruitment & Selection
- Presentation to be written
- CD-ROM (QuickGuides)

Project Management
- Presentation to be written

Objective-Setting
- Presentation to be written

Influencing Skills
- Presentation to be written
- CD-ROM (Tarragon) – Negotiate for a Positive Outcome
- Video – From No to Yes

Basics of Finance
- Presentation to be written

Time Management
- Presentation to be written
- CD-ROM (Maxim) – Manage Time for Better Results

Making the Right Decision
- Presentation to be written
- CD-ROM (Maxim) – Making the Right Decision

Interpersonal Skills
- Presentation to be written
- CD-ROMs
  - (Tarragon) – Listening Effectively
  - (ITC) – Interpersonal Skills
  - (Aziz) – Perfect Presenter
  - (BBC) – Right First Time
- Videos exist
  - Good Question
  - Straight Talking: The Art of Assertiveness

Coaching/Mentoring
- Presentation to be written
- CD-ROMs
  - (Xebec) – Coaching for Results
  - (Harvard) – High Performance Management

Leading Teams
- Presentation to be written
- CD-ROMs
  - (Xebec) – Leading Teams
  - (Tarragon) – Dealing with Conflict

Change Management
- Presentation to be written
- CD-ROM (Harvard) – Realising Change

CLIFFORD CHANCE

Background

Clifford Chance is one of the leading international law firms in the world. The firm employs 6,000 people worldwide, of whom some 2,500 work in the London office (www.cliffordchance. com).

In early 1999 a newly appointed director of human resources initiated a review of the firm's human resource strategy. One of the conclusions was that although the existing training courses (technical, managerial and interpersonal skills) were well regarded, they were perceived to be predominantly focused towards the London office. Staff outside London considered themselves at a disadvantage in terms of access.

At this time the HR director restructured the human resource department. He created three divisions: resourcing, personnel operations and a development division – this last embraced training courses provision, career and performance management, and a new initiative for online training.

Defining the objective

Previously Clifford Chance had established a library of training materials on both CD-ROMs and books. For a period a designated PC had been made available to use these materials. Utilisation had, however, been sporadic and there had been limited linkages with other learning and training initiatives. Available programmes were not geared to a law firm and people did not find the time to access the material.

On the positive side, however, two features of Clifford Chance's infrastructure suggested that online learning could offer an attractive option. First, the firm was developing an intranet and using the site for a variety of internal purposes. Second, there was extensive management information available in-house to assist lawyers to add value to their clients.

Clifford Chance faced a challenge that could be articulated in a deceptively simple fashion. The objective was to create an online learning system, delivered through the intranet, which offered similar opportunities for access throughout the world and built on the firm's existing training programmes and knowledge base.

Developing the options

What was required was an arrangement that would permit the existing Clifford Chance training modules to be customised for the intranet. In the words of Peter Carrick, who had taken on the role of structuring and implementing the online training initiative, the immediate problem was to identify:

> someone who would enter into partnership with Clifford Chance to design a specific system which would allow us to author courses.

The identification of an effective authoring tool was seen as essential. The firm had looked at off-the-shelf programmes available on CD-ROM and accessed through the firm's intranet. Some were considered to be of good educational quality – but these were expensive. A suite of specialised financial training courses had been well received, but even these were not specifically geared to lawyers, still less to the specific needs of Clifford Chance.

The firm recognised that it would benefit from the introduction of a tracking system at a later stage in the implementation process. This would monitor individual usage and permit the effective recording and monitoring of training. However, the short-term requirement was the need to have course material on the intranet.

One set of discussions took place with a leading supplier of learning systems (see page 44 for a definition of the term). The system on offer was extensive in its functionality and would require a considerable financial commitment. Examination and review suggested that this was not an appropriate option. The learning system would offer an attractive method of launching existing material through the intranet (and tracking usage), but the urgent need for Clifford Chance was to develop materials to launch. Moreover, it was concluded that there could be difficulties in gaining cultural acceptance and that the e-learning system would work best when people were used to distance-learning materials and where a library of extensive materials (whether internally generated or generic material purchased from outside) was already in use.

The second broad option was therefore to construct, in partnership, an appropriate authoring facility whereby Clifford Chance could develop its own suites of intranet-delivered material. In training terms this was an attractive option. Not only would it allow worldwide access but it would permit immediate updating – a vital facility in the fast-moving world of commercial law. This would also embed links with the information management system.

Clifford Chance had already reviewed the options and authoring products. Two important conclusions emerged from the early analysis. First, many of the acceptable tools available were designed to assist web design in general – they were not specifically designed for training needs, though some could be readily adapted for this purpose. Second, whatever tool was chosen, Clifford Chance would need to enter an arrangement with a software specialist who would assist with the customisation and implementation.

After reviewing three alternative tools, the chosen approach was to use tools developed by Macromedia, a large California-headquartered software house specialising in websites and interactive media. The best option seemed to be a relatively straightforward website development tool, called Dreamweaver, to which could be added a supplementary product called Coursebuilder. This latter product would facilitate interactive learning, offering multiple choice and selection options. There would also be the opportunity for adding further multimedia options over time. In due course another product may be introduced to permit tracking of course usage.

Looking forward

Once a decision had been made to use this option, the software house who had developed Clifford Chance's intranet was asked to assist in implementation. This will involve preparing templates for each training module and developing the links with the firm's library of know-how and precedents. The first two modules currently under design are Legal Writing and Professional Ethics and Standards. Both are firmly embedded in Clifford Chance's business approach.

Clifford Chance's initiative has benefited from a clear goal at the start. So far, expensive mistakes have been avoided, in particular the purchase of an attractive but inappropriate system. Current challenges can be divided into two: implementation and acceptability. Clearly the software solution will need to be robust, and results from the pilot will be closely scrutinised. The second challenge, of acceptability, is one that all training professionals face – how will this new approach be received by the extensive numbers of capable and articulate staff for whose ultimate benefit it is designed?

My thanks to Peter Carrick for his assistance in the preparation of this case study.

Case Study

THE POST OFFICE

Background

The Post Office is one of the UK's biggest organisations: it employs around 200,000 staff, it achieved sales in 1999/2000 of over £7.5 billion, and is a well-known and trusted brand.

It is undergoing, and will continue to undergo, massive change. In 1998 a major reorganisation took place that created 17 business units: these include market-facing and service delivery activities, as well as support services. The drivers for change include legislation, liberalisation of the market, regulatory issues and increased competition internationally and from the connected economy.

The Post Office has many strengths, but cultural change is essential for survival. Its brands are strong and those staff who interact with the public are generally valued and respected. Customer complaints often reflect problems with operating systems: lost letters and parcels, for example. Generally, however, there is a need for the organisation to become more market-focused and customer- and client-sensitive. Evidently training and development are at the heart of this change process, but will the connectivity and web-based training assist? The two illustrations below demonstrate the current position at The Post Office. Based on past experience and current priorities, a number of possibilities are under review.

Training Royal Mail staff
The majority of staff employed by The Post Office are in the core letter service: they undertake collection, sorting and delivery of letters and small parcels. There are around 160,000 employees involved in performing these services, with another 9,500 managers also employed by the Royal Mail. As would be expected, these employees are distributed around the country, reflecting the spread of the nation's population. There are, for example, some 1,500 area offices where the mail is sorted before it is delivered to the home.

Each year some 13,000 new entrants join the workforce. There is a commitment to give every joiner induction from day one: three days are spent in the classroom and two days receiving appropriate on-the-job training. This induction training must always be given top priority: any performance deficiencies could lead to customer complaints and expensive reworking.

Induction training is followed by a range of work area training activities. Traditionally, these could involve health and safety and lifting and handling. Recently, however, there has been a shift to more customer-focused activities reflecting the changing skill set required by all front-line staff.

A further issue, which is rising up the agenda, concerns the need to prepare suitable postmen and postwomen for their first front-line management post. In the view of Helen Rolph, the Royal Mail's head of training, the gap between the skills required to perform front-line duties and those required to manage the people who perform them is widening: on promotion, employees must be assisted to acquire both computer skills and interpersonal skills to fulfil their new role.

Training for Royal Mail staff to date has been delivered by experienced trainers in the classroom. In the 1980s and early 1990s, The Post Office invested in customised interactive video, but this was not well supported and did not have a significant impact. In 1998 six pilot learning centres were opened in different parts of the country. These were aimed at front-line staff, they were free at point of use (though staff had to come in their own time), and their opening times were such that there was some access across all three shifts operating in the course of the working day. Computer-based packages were available, together with other training resources. Someone was on hand to assist learners when required. These centres were deemed to be successful where they were actively marketed.

Current Royal Mail priorities on training lie elsewhere, however, and there are no immediate intentions to extend the learning centre network. The main focus is an ambitious and challenging project entitled 'Work-time Learning'. This commits the Royal Mail to ensure that all front-line staff receive 30 minutes' learning per week. This will be delivered by the line manager at the place of work, during slack time. There is a need for upfront training for the first line managers and for ongoing support for them: it is essentially a coaching model of group learning led by front-line managers.

Helen Rolph argues that she would 'love to be able to find some technology which could support or assist that training'. However, she can identify a number of problems that must be overcome. First, any material must be suitable for The Post Office; generic technology-based training material has not been found to gain acceptability in the past. Second, there must be an acceptable business case for the intervention. Third, there must be an acceptable delivery channel. Fourth, it must be acceptable in the culture.

There is evidence that such possibilities are emerging. Delivery offices, for example, are making increased use of The Post Office intranet for information on work practices. It is not a big step to extend this to training and to widen access to front-line staff. Helen Rolph feels, however, that the most promising opportunities for the use of e-learning could well lie in the support and development of new front-line managers. Motivation is high amongst this population and if learning using technology was perceived to be part of the new skill set required, it would have ready acceptability. Suitable generic material would need to be supplemented by specific information on Royal Mail practices. Coaching support could also be needed for those involved, so the resource commitment could be considerable.

Senior management development

The cultural change must operate at all levels, but the development of an effective cohort of the most senior employees ranks very high on the agenda. Traditionally, the way to success was seen as being able to operate as an effective administrator. In the past, this has led to a tendency to over-process, over-engineer and to play safe. In the words of Jill Garraway, head of senior management development, 'Anyone who is gritty or difficult tends to get a black mark – yet we need people who will challenge the status quo.'

Jill currently has strategic responsibility for the top 150 people. She also has the objective of identifying talented staff at lower levels and promoting their development.

Her main priority is the creation of a framework for senior management development. This will be a structural approach to retain, motivate and develop through key enablers. It embraces reward and compensation, performance objectives (what to do, not how to do it), the creation of headroom and transparency of information.

She also needs to restructure a suite of three management courses. These are a business leader seminar (four days), a business management programme (10 days) and a management development programme (10 days). Between the events, there are development workshops with an action learning element. These workshops are in need of updating: in Jill Garraway's words, there is a dated feel about them and 'a lot of people have been through the sheep dip'.

Given this clear set of priorities, how can e-learning assist? There are two firm projects at the proposal stage.

The first concerns the use of psychometric testing over the intranet as a way of identifying and assessing talent. This has the dual advantages of accessibility and transparency. Discussions are taking place with The Post Office's psychologists. There do not appear to be technical problems with this approach, and the intranet site is well embedded. The practical questions concern the need for face-to-face support, from someone with the appropriate skills, to deal with the sensitive issues that will arise.

The second priority concerns the suite of senior-level courses. Jill Garraway is looking for appropriate products that will offer what she describes as 'e-substitute'. This will be a form of interactive learning that will keep people up to date while developing knowledge. It will save time and improve cost-effectiveness. The Post Office will not, however, seek to develop this product: they are confident with the way that the market is moving that appropriate offerings from a quality business school will appear. This will be a supplement, a part substitution but not a total replacement for classroom initiatives.

A common feature of all the elements in The Post Office's approach is a shift of responsibility towards the learner. It also requires a general acceptance of technology-based initiatives. The former is accelerating a cultural change that was started with a shift in responsibility for career development. The latter is more of a challenge, but is regarded as inevitable.

My thanks to Jill Garraway and Helen Rolph for their assistance with this case study.

Case Study

IBM'S GLOBAL E-LEARNING MODEL

Background
In 1997 IBM undertook a global benchmark study to determine its approach to the delivery of training using technological enablers. It found that two models were predominant at the time.

The first involved the transfer of appropriate topics to computer-based training, then using mainly CD-ROMs. Typical topics (or subjects on the training curriculum) to be transferred would generally be chosen from the IT curriculum: JavaScript or HTML for example. These were thought to be 'suitable' for this approach.

The second model was to take a whole course and shift its contents to the Web or CD-ROM. Such courses could involve both knowledge or skills elements. The courses selected would either be high-profile events or events that had a large course throughput.

Nancy Lewis, head of global management development, felt that neither model was appropriate for the learning needs of the 30,000 IBM staff worldwide. Instead, IBM took a decision to develop and deliver its own solution. It approached the problem from the perspective of curriculum design. What were the appropriate training methods or training media to be used for each learning objective?

The model
After detailed exploration, IBM developed a four-tier model called (ahead of its time) the e-learning model. The tiers were in turn:

- information and awareness
- understanding and beginning of practice
- collaborative learning
- face-to-face intervention.

Delivering learning through this model demands the consideration of the most effective approach at each stage and the deliberate and systematic orchestration of training throughout.

At the first introductory tier (information and awareness), the approach used is to put information on the Web. Summaries of best practice and just-in-time performance support tools are available in this form. Best thinking on over 40 leadership and people management topics of concern to managers are available, including materials from Harvard Business School Publishing. These are supplemented with the regular publication of *Management Quickview*. Nancy Lewis emphasises that no first stage briefing should be longer than 12 pages.

The next tier – the understanding of best practice – involves the use of immersive simulation tools delivered through the intranet. These are scenario-based and different approaches are used depending on whether a person has a left brain or right brain preference. (The left brain is considered analytic in approach and those with this preference prefer a step-by-step sequential format. The right brain is more creative, complex and fanciful.)

The third tier involves the creation of a virtual classroom, with peer group discussion using the Lotus Learning Space Groupware (see page 74 for a definition of the term). Here managers learn teaming skills, and create and build real-life networks while enhancing IBM's intellectual capital.

The fourth and highest tier brings learners into the classroom for face-to-face discussion. The other three tiers are used before and also after the classroom to reinforce learning. Certain basic subjects may not involve learning input beyond the second tier. In Nancy Lewis's words, the tiered approach 'begs you to think what you are doing at each level'. Importantly e-learning does not eliminate face-to-face education – it enhances it.

Applying the model
Application of the model must be seen as a continuous process, with many learning activities extending over 12 months.

Subject matter experts in any part of IBM can use the model to develop and distribute content. It allows the company to integrate and share training across the world. In May 2000 IBM formed a special business unit called IBM Mindspan to offer its solution externally.

In conclusion IBM believes that the introduction of its global e-learning model has acted as a powerful signal of its commitment to its staff. It is seen as an investment in people and a tool for retention.

Further information on IBM's approach to embedding learning is contained in the next chapter, where time and space to learn is discussed.

My thanks to Nancy Lewis, head of global management development, IBM, for her assistance in the preparation of this case study.

Chapter 5

Focusing on the learner

It's déjà vu *all over again*

This chapter considers the issues involved in learner support in the age of e-learning. The central argument that runs throughout this consideration is summarised in the following proposition.

Proposition 14

A new discipline of learner support will emerge and should be encouraged.

The change in emphasis from training to learning was considered in Chapter 3 and hopefully should be recognised as marking a major shift of focus for the training professional. Improvements in technology, and particularly the emergence of connectivity, offer the trainer an unprecedented opportunity to deliver interventions that are designed around the needs of the learner. To return to the vocabulary of Internet business, these can become customer-centric offerings. The learning experience can be tailored to the individual learner's requirements and preferences. The importance of this change in emphasis cannot be overstated. It has led to the emergence of the new paradigm of learner-centred interventions introduced at the end of Chapter 3 (page 70).

The quote at the beginning of this chapter is Yogi Berra's 'It's *déjà vu* all over again.' To an extent we are revisiting old territory: we are asking how we can encourage and assist people to learn. There is a considerable body of research and extensive literature on this subject and some of the most important strands are reviewed later in this chapter. This material, mainly drawn from US writers, is quite theoretical and will prove more demanding for the reader than much of the discussion so far. It is an aspect of the potential of e-learning that will take us nearer to the boundaries of what is known.

These conceptual frameworks for learning must, however, be considered in the next context. So far it has been suggested that a quarter of training content could be provided through e-learning. This must necessarily alter the approach to learner support required in the organisation. Many of the practical issues of implementation will be considered in the next chapter. To set the scene, the place of learner support is illustrated in Figure 13.[1]

‘There is a danger of being seduced by the technology’

Figure 13 portrays the intervention that a trainer makes in the organisation as three corners of a triangle. Learning needs should continue to be the starting point: nothing has changed here. The second apex – the platform for delivery – has been dramatically affected by the new technology, which offers exciting opportunities. Regrettably, to date most of the debate has concentrated on these opportunities: to re-emphasise the point made in Proposition 4 (page

Figure 13
ISSUES IN E-LEARNING

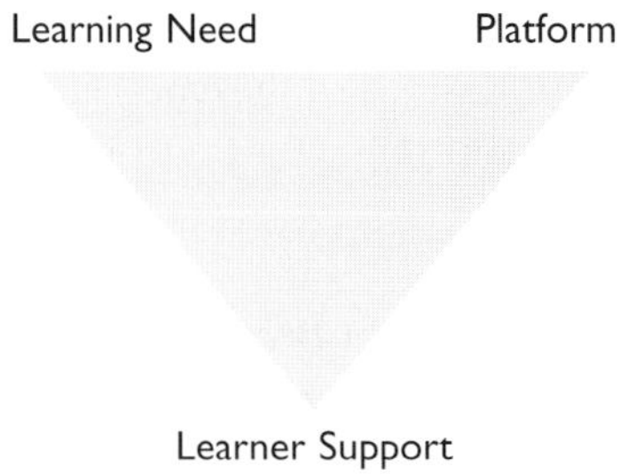

Learning Need   Platform

Learner Support

Learning Need – This should drive the whole process, but new business models have produced a new agenda and new training needs. Identifying training needs remains critical.

Platform – The new technology (Internet/intranet/Web) offers an exciting platform, particularly when used in conjunction with course-based training and experiential learning

Learner Support – (Coaching, mentoring, etc) must be supplied appropriately. It will be affected by both learning needs and technology. Adequate provision of learner support is the responsibility of the learning and development profession.

42), there is a danger of being seduced by the technology. It is the opportunity for improved learning that the technology creates that is important. If these exciting opportunities are to be realised, appropriate support for the learner is needed. These issues – described as learner support and outlined at the lowest point of the triangle in Figure 13 – form the subject of this chapter.

A new term is introduced here to describe some of the activities involved in learner support: that term is 'soft technology'[2] and is outlined in Focus Point 16. It can be seen from this Focus Point that a broad definition of soft technology is proposed and will be used for the remainder of the book. At its narrowest, the definition could refer to the architecture of the learning material (or how easy it is to navigate and assimilate information). The definition adopted will extend to wider organisational issues, including the steps taken to promote, encourage and facilitate access.

Using this wide definition, appropriate soft technology is required to implement the exciting opportunities created by the hard technology. Learner support describes the activities undertaken by the human resource professional to ensure that people learn effectively. In the next chapter it is argued that the underlying skill set will redefine the roles of many trainers. In this chapter we consider some of the issues involved in learner support. Be warned: the news is not always good. It is possible to identify many of the questions, but so far the profession has come up with few of the answers.

Connectivity and the classroom

A useful starting point in identifying some of the significant issues involved in learning in the new context is to ask what is special about classroom learning. Learners and trainers instinctively opt for this method of instruction, certainly for interpersonal skills training. Pete Weaver, the senior vice president of the management development consultancy Development Dimensions International (DDI), has offered an analysis that is reproduced as Focus Point 17.

‘The arrival of the mobile phone is the biggest assault to date on the training room’

Focus Point 16: Soft technology

The concept of soft technology is one that is emerging in speeches, commentary and literature.

In April 1999, for example, Sir John Daniel, Vice Chancellor of the Open University, who attributed much of the university's success to soft technology, included the following outline in a speech:

> The key technology for the mega-universities is not any particular device. It is the increasingly organised body of knowledge called distance education. *Distance education uses a combination of hard and soft technologies. Hard technologies are bits and bytes, electrons and pixels, satellites and search engines. Soft technologies are processes, approaches, sets of rules and models of organisations.* [Current author's italics.] The most important thing to understand about using distance education for university-level teaching and learning that is both intellectually powerful and competitively cost-effective is that you must concentrate on getting the soft technologies right. The hard technologies change. Indeed, they change rapidly.

> These soft technologies are simply the working practices that underpin the rest of today's modern and industrial service economy: division of labour, specialisation, teamwork and project management. [www.open.ac.uk/vcs-speeches]

The important issue here is the valuable distinction between hard and soft technology. This will be used throughout this book in the following sense:

Hard technology refers to the information and communication technology systems. Figure 3 (page 45) considered the architecture of these systems as applied to learning.

Soft technology will hereafter refer to the activities that must be taken at all levels in an organisation to embed that hard technology effectively.

All of his points have some resonance for the training manager. In addition, getting people together in a classroom can have cultural benefits for the organisation. They learn from each other and can gain reassurance from the fact that they face the same problems. Unfortunately, the improved communications associated with the connected economy does diminish the third bullet point in Focus

Focus Point 17: A bias for the classroom?

🖉 People are social learners; they enjoy an exchange of ideas with others and like the support of other learners.

🖉 Some people need learning tension. People often go to classroom events (and remain there) because their absence is conspicuous. However, with e-learning the feeling of anonymity is often commensurate with a lack of commitment.

🖉 There is a separation from interruptions; if people are in the classroom the primary focus of their activity is clear, and colleagues and subordinates are less likely to offer distractions.

🖉 There is a change in atmosphere; not only is there a release from telephone interruptions but it is possible to create a mood that is less frenetic and is conducive to reflection.

🖉 There is a sense of self-worth; in many instances being sent away on a course is seen as an indication that an organisation is willing to invest in an individual.

🖉 There is a management bias: senior managers understand the financial model involved in classroom training. E-learning (with its heavy upfront investment) does not command the same support. The Web has led managers to expect content to be free.

My thanks to Pete Weaver for permission to reproduce his work (www.ddiworld.com).

Point 17: separation from interruptions. Unless this author's experience is unique, the arrival of the mobile phone is the biggest assault to date on the training room, with Internet access through hotel switchboards a close second. The imminent convergence of mobile telephones and the Internet is to be dreaded greatly by classroom instructors.

‘ e-learning cannot replicate all the facets that make classroom training popular ’

Connectivity, therefore, can be regarded as both a threat and an opportunity for effective organisational learning. The main thrust of this chapter is that it is the training professional's responsibility to understand what is at issue in his or her organisation. How do individuals learn what they need or wish to learn? This question can be answered in two ways: first, by gaining a theoretical grounding and considering preferences, styles and motivation; second, by continually gathering information from learning in the organisation. What should be gained from this brief overview of the classroom is that e-learning cannot (certainly at present) replicate all the facets that make classroom training popular and well established.

Frameworks in training and education

A valuable commentary on conceptual issues underlying learning is offered by Marcy Driscoll, Professor of Instructional Systems and Educational Psychology at Florida State University. Her book, *Psychology of Learning for Instruction*, applies learning theories to the practical issues involved in effective instructional design.

She considers learning and defines it as a persisting change in performance or performance potential that results from experience or interaction with the world. A learning theory, then, is a set of constructs linking observed changes in performance with what is thought to bring about those changes. Instruction is about the deliberate arrangement of learning conditions to promote the attaining of some intended goal; an instructional theory can provide principles by which teachers and instructional designers can assure learning.[3] (p345)

The theoretical analysis can be extended by distinguishing between two major frameworks:

- ✐ One framework considers how content and knowledge is *transmitted* for the learner.
- ✐ A second framework considers how the learner *transforms* information, generates hypotheses and makes decisions about the content and knowledge.

At a crude level the former can be characterised as an instructor-centred approach and the latter as a learner-centred approach. Neither framework should be regarded as preferable. Those responsible for training must consider all aspects of effective design. In Proposition 6 (page 54) it was argued that the distinction between learning and training is of value and should be maintained. Using this distinction, the first framework can be regarded as a training framework and the second as a learning framework.

A most effective analysis of the value of an approach that considers frameworks was developed by Zane Berge, a US writer in the field of learning technology. The discussion that follows immediately is drawn from his analysis.[4]

One of the key concepts in a *transmission* framework is that a teacher can pass on a fixed body of information. The student or learner interacts with pre-packaged content. The skill of the teacher lies in the selection of the content and in teaching style to produce a specific outcome from the students.

Transformation frameworks necessarily emphasise individual thinking and construction of meaning. Training under this approach is more tentative, flexible and experimental – hence it is student- or learner-centred. In this context a community of learners will improve learning through their interaction.

Berge is interested in the practical issues involved in developing an effective model for distance education and training in the organisation:

> The biggest differences in various models of distance education center around the assumptions underlying the educational philosophy of the model builder. Some models are designed for industrialized or pre-packaged knowledge ... others are more flexible, customized to the individual and organic ...

> While there are many variations of distance training mainly differing by the types of technology used ... basically the difference rests in the control aspect. In some models, the trainer and the organization have primary control, and in others control resides with the trainee...A second dimension involves whether or not the model used involves distributing instruction to groups of participants at a given place or is designed for individual participation with some type of asynchronous communication medium being used.[4] (p24)

The term 'synchronous' (and its antonym 'asynchronous') is used frequently in discussions on distance learning. A definition is offered in Focus Point 18.

Some readers may regard this discussion as too theoretical. It is worth remembering, however, that in the USA the discipline of

Focus Point 18: Synchronous and asynchronous learning

The distinction is simple:

🖎 *Sychronous* learning is real-time learning that takes place when all participants are involved at the same time. Recipients of synchronous learning need not be in the same place: two-way video, for example, is synchronous and allows interaction between student and teacher.

🖎 *Asynchronous* learning occurs when content is built at one time but accessed at another. It is 'time-shifted' and can allow learners access at their own convenience. Common content can be prepared and delivered when needed (possibly just in time).

The above are the author's own distinctions to emphasise the difference from the training manager's perspective. A more precise definition embedded in the technology of distance learning and education is available in Berge and Schreiber.[4] (pp411–8)

instructional systems development (ISD) is underpinned by a solid theoretical base. That base takes into account both transmission and transformation frameworks. The result is an emphasis on the design of effective instructional material. It would be a tragedy if, in the rush to implement e-learning, an inappropriate product was produced and delivered because basic distinctions were lost. Both Berge and Driscoll's works are well worth reading if this danger is to be avoided.

To introduce a lighter note, another insight to be gained from reading Berge is his introduction of Thornburg's engaging categorisation of venues for learning. These are set out in Focus Point 19.

> ‹How can the information gained from the campfire and watering-hole be captured and shared?›

Thornburg's primordial metaphors should be helpful whenever e-learning is implemented. What are the possibilities and problems in

Focus Point 19: Venues for learning

David Thornburg[5] introduces the idea of three venues for learning, drawn from primordial metaphors.

Campfires: for thousands of years storytelling around the campfire has been used as an occasion when people sit at the foot of the elders and become informed. This sharing of knowledge, skills and wisdom continues to be a critical element in teaching and learning.

The watering-hole: this is different in that, historically, people shared information with neighbours who just happened to be there. This is more informal and haphazard, with stimulating exchanges and gossips. The essence is a shared culture and social learning.

The cave: this is a secluded personal space where a person can take what has been learned from others and make sense of it. Knowledge or insights are internalised or made one's own in this space.

One other useful metaphor is suggested by Thornburg's classification.

The hunting expedition: here a group embark on a task together and their skills and capabilities are exposed to the outside world. Individuals can learn from each other, a process that is particularly effective if the more experienced are aware of their need to assist the less experienced.

delivering content to the cave and in facilitating learning on the hunting expedition? How can the information gained from the campfire and watering-hole be captured and shared? These issues are central to learner support. Readers may also wish to reflect on their own preferred venue for learning. Mine is a cave in Norfolk where I read, reflect and write while my wife travels to the nearest market town to hunt mammoth for dinner.

Learning preferences and styles

There is an evident link here with individual learning preferences. People learn in different ways and one of the skills of successful

teaching is to adapt the approach to the individual. The most successful model in the UK was that developed and popularised by
Peter Honey and Alan Mumford. This drew, in part, from the work
of David Kolb, an American academic and consultant.[6]

Kolb introduced the concept of the learning cycle: at stage one a
person starts off with an experience; stage two of the cycle is to
observe and reflect on that experience; stage three is to develop certain principles and concepts from that reflection; stage four is to test
these principles and concepts either by replicating the initial experience or by trying out the principles in new circumstances. This will
produce a new experience (stage one again) and the cycle continues.
Some advocates of this approach would suggest that the individual's
experience of the learning cycle could also be parallelled in the
organisation. In this case it is particularly important that the organisation ensures that there is adequate opportunity for stages two and
three of the cycle (respectively called 'systematic reflection' and
'abstract conceptualisation') to take place.

Honey and Mumford's contribution was to postulate how a learning
cycle could be used to identify individual learning styles. For them
all the evidence suggested that individuals have learning styles. In
the early 1980s they published a manual of learning styles that
included a most useful and practical questionnaire; this was updated
and reissued in 2000.[7, 8]

In his current thinking, Peter Honey offers the following seven assertions about learning:

- Learning is both a process and an outcome. We use the same
  word to describe both aspects. Some confusion can arise and we
  are generally much more comfortable talking about the outcome
  than concentrating on the process.
- Learning is not just about knowledge. It is also about skills,
  insights, beliefs, values, attitudes, habits, feelings, wisdom,
  shared understanding and self-awareness. It covers a multitude of
  things.
- Learning outcomes can be desirable or undesirable for the learner
  and for others.
- Learning processes can be conscious or unconscious. People can

learn when they do not realise they are learning and certainly can learn as an incidental result of other activity.

✍ Conscious learning processes can be proactive or reactive. A lot of learning can be reflective after the event, but we can set ourselves goals or objectives that will assist.

✍ The learning process occurs inside the individual, but making the outcomes explicit, and sharing them with others, adds value to the learning.

✍ There is no one right way to learn for everybody and for every situation.

The last of these assertions brings us to the heart of Honey and Mumford's contribution: learning style is about preference. Peter Honey's favoured term is 'learning style preferences'.

Honey and Mumford's approach is illustrated in Figure 14.

The lower-case letters in Figure 14 describe the learning cycle. Learners may start from any one of the four elements. Each element

Figure 14
THE LEARNING CYCLE

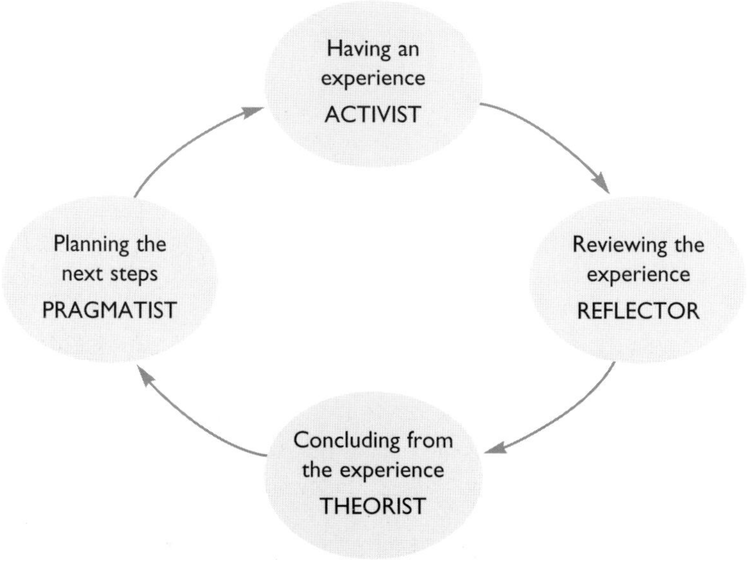

Reproduced with permission from Peter Honey Learning

contributes to an interactive learning process. The upper-case letters are descriptions of four learning style preferences associated in turn with each element of the cycle. In summary:

- *Activists* like to take direct action, are enthusiastic and welcome new challenges and experiences. They are primarily interested in the here and now and less interested in putting things into a broader context.
- *Reflectors* like to think about things in detail before taking action. They take a thoughtful approach and are good listeners. They will welcome the opportunity to repeat a piece of learning.
- *Theorists* like to see how things fit into a pattern. They are logical, objective, systems people who prefer a sequential approach to problems, are analytical, pay great attention to detail and tend to be perfectionists.
- *Pragmatists* like to see how things work in practice and enjoy experimenting with new ideas. They are practical, down to earth and like solving problems. They appreciate the opportunity to try out what they have learned.

This is a rich and helpful analysis with evident practical implications for learners and trainers.

Learners who are aware of their preferences can select learning opportunities that match their style preferences. They can seek (and be assisted) to become balanced learners by strengthening underutilised preferences. Trainers as enablers of learning can make the whole learning process explicit and can use learning style preferences to encourage group learning activity.

‘The central questions for the training professional remain unchanged’

The platform for the delivery of training will change with the arrival of the Internet. However, the central questions for the training professional remain unchanged: how do people learn best and how can we help people to learn more effectively? An appreciation of the theoretical frameworks provides a helpful background from which to work. A consideration of learning styles offers one useful area of insight. Other issues concern motivation (which will be considered next) and, to reflect on Thornburg's categorisation set out in Focus Point 19, time and space to learn. All can be brought together in the next proposition.

Proposition 15

There will be a renewed interest in learner motivation, learning styles and time and space to learn.

Motivation to learn

That high motivation on the part of the student is an important enabler for learning can be readily accepted. To illustrate, at Ernst & Young there are three occasions when individuals display a singular thirst for knowledge:

- when they have just joined the organisation and are eager to gain the background information needed to make a contribution and gain the respect and confidence of their colleagues
- when they are nearing the time of professional examinations that will give them valued qualifications
- when they are approaching partner admission and need to satisfy the requirements of a demanding assessment centre.

Nothing else quite captures the energy displayed around these decisions – which are related to events with clear paybacks for positive results.

Alas, not all learning events have such an immediate payback, but there is plenty of information and guidance available to suggest ways of improving motivation. Learner motivation is something that the training manager can influence. Marcy Driscoll's work on learning theory was discussed earlier in this chapter. In her book, *Psychology of Learning for Instruction*, she offers the following analysis of the main sources of motivation to learn:[3] (p306ff)

- curiosity and interest
- goals and goal orientation
- self-efficacy beliefs (the ability to organise and execute the causes of action required to produce given attainments).

These factors all relate to the individual's motivation to learn before the learning has actually begun and during a learning event. Other factors concern the learner's continued desire to study or participate. This aspect is about the skills required to monitor progress and achieve self-regulation.

Stimulating motivation through effective instructional strategy is the subject of a whole number of texts – mainly produced by American authors. As well as the volume by Marcy Driscoll already cited,[3] a book by Professor Raymond J. Wlodkowski is recommended.[9]

It should not be forgotten that one way of improving learner motivation could be to identify and remove barriers to learning. There are many reasons why individuals could prefer not to learn. Some will be specific to the situation in the organisation, but a general list would include:

- avoidance, fear of demonstrating a lack of skill or competence
- a general lack of awareness of the need to develop or the opportunities available
- blaming others for inadequate performance or capability rather than taking responsibility for own actions or feelings
- lack of personal confidence
- a general belief that people cannot change.[10]

Time and space to learn

The third element of Proposition 15 concerns individual preferences: where and when do people learn best? Considering how important this is to the future of e-learning, there is a paucity of general research information on the subject – let alone information specific to an organisation.

For example, in the early 1990s the CD-ROM emerged as the preferred tool for technology-based training (see Focus Point 11, page 36). There was a movement to establish learning resource centres that would contain libraries of CD-ROMs and other distance-learning materials. Vendors of multimedia training tools gave added momentum to the movement by offering special discounts on training materials or, in some cases, an outsourced management arrangement.

The two case studies set out at the end of this chapter demonstrate that there is much to be said for dedicated facilities where staff can access learning materials. Both British Airways, in reassessing its QUEST and communication points, and Motorola, in developing its learning strategy at its corporate university, are reviewing the place of learning centres. They have adopted different but considered approaches.

Generally, there is an embarrassing lack of published information on the use and acceptability of learning resource centres. Enquirers are left with a distinct feeling that they may not have been successful – appealing only to a minority of potential users and contributing little to organisational objectives. Many may have been quietly forgotten. Training managers are good at burying their dead ideas: they are not so good at organising (still less publicising) the memorial service.

Returning to the main theme of time and space to learn, some recent research has been undertaken by Elliott Masie, of the Masie Center in the USA, whose contribution was introduced in Chapter 2. He carried out a short survey entitled 'Learning at our busy desks'.[11] The survey was delivered electronically and the sample was drawn from the 3,000 respondents who receive his regular e-mailed newsletter. However, despite limitations of the sample population, it does offer some useful results and these are summarised in Focus Point 20.

The clear preference from this survey is for working at the desk in the organisation's time. This obviously raises some problems in ensuring that the necessary privacy is assured. Interestingly, some manufacturers of office furniture are addressing the issue by designing furniture that allows screens or pods to be put in place.

Commenting on the results, Elliott Masie has introduced the concept of organisational surround. His argument is that course-based training invariably begins with a 'drum roll'. Participants arrive, the door is closed, they write their names on a badge or name tent. This is generally followed by introductions and an opening ritual (a favourite is to ask participants whether they are volunteers, sceptics or hostages at the course; this is commended as a way of teasing out the dissidents). The instructor then proceeds.

Focus Point 20: Learning at desks: a summary of survey results

If you were about to participate in an important learning activity, where would you want to do it?

Results:	at my desk	47 per cent
	in a conference room/learning centre	
	at work	30 per cent
	at home	21 per cent
	on the road	1 per cent
	on a bus or a train whilst commuting	1 per cent

If you were to take this class at your desk, when would you most likely take it?

Results:	during work	49 per cent
	before work	16 per cent
	after work	17 per cent
	at lunch	16 per cent
	on my days off	2 per cent

Results from those people who had an office with a door, or work as a trainer, indicated a more positive response to working at the desk.

(Reproduced with permission and thanks to the Masie Center)

This 'drum roll' signals a change in atmosphere. Participants are there to learn – even in the age of mobile technology, concentration can be guaranteed for the first 10 minutes. Other members of staff are expected to respect the fact that the course member is off-site and unavailable.

> *If e-learning is to be effective, it must take place in an appropriate organisational surround*

E-learning does not begin with an introductory drum roll. There are no shared rituals: there is no change in atmosphere. Elliott Masie argues powerfully that if e-learning is to be effective, it must take place in an appropriate organisational surround – this must involve physical signals to colleagues that learning is taking place. One obvious way of achieving this is to create special learning spaces or centres. Elliott Masie's view is that unless the learning centre is within close proximity and is available for 90-minute sessions without prior reservation, it is unlikely to offer an acceptable alternative to learning at the desk.

Learner acceptability: the IBM research

There is greater need for information, both generally and specific to the training manager's organisation, on all aspects of learning. A useful study undertaken by IBM Management Development offers insights on the acceptability of e-learning technology. This was reported in an edition of the American Society for Training and Development's journal.[12]

In a valuable article, Nancy Lewis and Peter Orton argued that at present many people do not understand enough about e-learning to be able to assess their preferences.

An exercise was undertaken at IBM using a technique known as conjoint analysis. Essentially this examines trade-offs to determine which combination of attributes is most satisfying to the customer. Conjoint analysis is a well-established consumer survey technique when the attributes are well understood: for example, house price against number of bedrooms. However, the exercise could not produce robust results:

> Knowledge learning preferences can inform instructional designs, but only if learners understand all of the variables and features. The current problem with learning interventions is that not all choices are salient to learners and, especially with online learning, not all attributes are understood.[12] (p47)

So far, encounters have been mixed:

> In fact, many users' experiences with online learning have been fraught with long download waits, choppy video, confusing navigation, and endless text screens. For some people, just having to install a plug-in can roadblock any sampling of online instruction.

Many, if not all, learners have scant knowledge of what a dynamic engaging online experience can be.[12] (p48)

IBM Management Development was faced with the problem of rolling out a new learning intervention, Basic Blue for Managers. This intervention involved 50 weeks on e-learning. IBM commissioned Professor Moon of Harvard Business School to assess general preferences for different approaches to delivering learning. A random sample of 63 new IBM managers was surveyed by questionnaire. Despite their high level of technology awareness, new IBM managers reported a preference for classroom learning over online learning (the term used in the survey).

However, when Professor Moon conducted post-programme interviews she found that respondents commended both approaches to learning – classroom and online – with equal enthusiasm. Moreover, to quote from the article:

> Most telling was that all respondents answered that they preferred learning the informational material (the cognitive-based development) online from their home or office rather than in a classroom setting.

> Conversely, the managers preferred learning the behavioural-skills material in a classroom environment rather than in an online setting . . . (p48)

Professor Moon concluded that after they had experienced online learning, respondents indicated they preferred an approach that was best suited to content. Key factors were the amount and type of material presented and the time available to review it:

> The key was the hybrid model. Rather than adopting a totally online program, they decided to take a best-of-both-worlds approach, and it really worked. (p49)

Learning in the new context

It is now appropriate to pull together the strands of this chapter. For the training profession the overall picture is depressing. We simply do not know what we need to know.

‹We simply do not know what
we need to know›

Few would disagree with the central argument and propositions set out in this chapter. The new technology offers the trainer the opportunity to deliver interventions to suit the learners' needs. This will result in the emergence of a new discipline of learner support. Knowledge on how people learn is essential for effective interventions. Such knowledge requires considered information on motivation, learning styles and preferences on time and space to learn.

Useful work has undoubtedly been undertaken on instructional development in the USA – and there is an extensive theoretical literature available on learning and training. The individuals and organisations cited in this chapter have all offered useful insights.

However, the stark truth is that e-learning takes place in a radically changed context from the classroom model. Although the questions to be asked may be the same, the answers could be very different. Much of the research base is inappropriate. Much of the academic research, for example, uses students for the 'sample participants'. Much of the data offered by vendors of products is specific to those products, and they are unlikely to wish to publicise failure.

Focus Point 21 sets out some simple questions that are central to learner support in any organisation. For those of us who are training

Focus Point 21: Learner support: the key questions

For each individual learner:

How do they prefer to learn?

✍ What is their learning style preference and what is the impact of e-learning on this style?

When do they prefer to learn?

✍ Do they prefer to learn in small bites or at an extended session?

Where do they prefer to learn?

✍ Do they prefer to learn at their desk, in specific rooms or spaces in the office or at home?

managers, this is what we need to know: the how, when and where preferences of learners in our organisations. The hope is that we can develop methodologies and share information.

In that spirit, an Ernst & Young questionnaire is included in Focus Point 22. This was designed to determine user reaction to a new learning portal. It offered individuals the chance to see what learning opportunities were available and to prepare a personal learning plan based on that information. Readers are welcome to adapt the questionnaire to their own needs.

References

1 My thanks to my colleague at Ernst & Young, Brenton Hague, who introduced me to the approach outlined in Figure 13.

2 I am grateful to Dr Michael Molenda, Associate Professor, Instructional Systems Technology, University of Indiana, for introducing me to the term soft technology and for his advice on its application. Like Daniel, he uses the term to refer to intellectual techniques and processes, although Molenda focuses more on processes related to instruction, such as instructional design. He also uses the term 'soft technologies of instruction' to refer to specific formats or templates that have been developed to hold various types of subject context.

3 DRISCOLL M. P. *Psychology of Learning for Instruction*. 2nd edn. Needham Heights, Mass., Allyn & Bacon, 2000.

4 BERGE Z. L. 'Conceptual frameworks in distance training and education'. In Berge Z. L. *and* Schreiber D. A. (EDS) *Distance Training*. San Francisco, Jossey-Bass, 1998. pp19–36.

5 THORNBURG D. D. 'Campfires in Cyberspace: Primordial metaphors for learning in the 21st century'. From www.tcpd.org/thornburg/handouts/Campfires.pdf.

6 KOLB D. *Experimental Learning*. Englewood Cliffs, Prentice Hall, 1984.

7 MUMFORD A. *Effective Learning*. London, Institute of Personnel and Development, 1999.

8 HONEY P. *and* MUMFORD A. *The Learning Styles Questionnaire* (80-item version). Maidenhead, Peter Honey Publications, 2000.

Focus Point 22: Ernst & Young questionnaire

Name   Office/Location

Department   Grade

L&D Manager

1 General reaction
How would you rate the potential overall value/usefulness of the portal?

No value   Very valuable

1   2   3   4   5   6   7   8   9   10

What could be done to improve its potential value/usefulness?

```
┌─────────────────────────────────────────────────┐
│                                                   │
│                                                   │
│                                                   │
│                                                   │
└─────────────────────────────────────────────────┘
```

2 General ease of use
Did you find it easy to navigate?

Very difficult   Very easy

1   2   3   4   5   6   7   8   9   10

```
┌─────────────────────────────────────────────────┐
│  Please provide examples of areas that were difficult to use. │
│                                                   │
│                                                   │
└─────────────────────────────────────────────────┘
```

Did you encounter any technology-related difficulties when using the portal?
For example, access, transferring information, speed of response.

None   Significant issues encountered

1   2   3   4   5   6   7   8   9   10

Please provide details below

Did you seek support to help you with any difficulties encountered?

Never   Frequently

1   2   3   4   5   6   7   8   9   10

Please provide examples of what support you needed and who you contacted.

3 Cultural feedback

How easy was it to find time to use the portal?

Did you primarily work in the office or at home when using the portal? Please provide a summary of when and where you used the portal.

4 Application

Did you construct a Personal Learning Plan? YES/NO

Please comment on your plan below. For example, how many different courses were included?

What did you do with your plan after its completion? Did you discuss it with your counselling manager/colleagues/L&D manager?

5 Future of the portal

What additional information/functionality would you like to see on the portal which could assist you in planning your learning?

6 Other comments

Please add other comments which you think would assist.

9   WLODKOWSKI R. J. *Enhancing Adult Motivation to Learn.* Revised edn. San Francisco, Jossey-Bass, 1999.

10 My thanks to Karen Jaques of Dove Nest for suggesting this aspect of improving motivation.

11 MASIE E. 'Learning at our busy desks'. *Learning Decisions*, May 2000.

12 LEWIS N. J. *and* ORTON P. 'The five attributes of innovative e-learning'. *Training and Development*, June 2000. pp47–51.

Case Study

LEARNING AT MOTOROLA UNIVERSITY – EMEA

Background
Motorola is a leading global company providing integrated com-munications solutions and embedded electronic solutions to its customers. It employs 140,000 worldwide. Motorola University (MU) was initially launched in the 1970s as the Motorola Training and Education Centre. Since then it has attracted much atten-tion, reflecting the growing interest in corporate universities (see pages 33–35). Motorola featured as a case study in the Government publication 'The future of corporate learning' (see Chapter 2, page 34).

This case concerns one aspect of MU's training activity: its approach to the implementation of technology-enabled learning for its 23,000 Europe, Middle East and Africa (EMEA) staff. Motorola's intention is to make 30 per cent of training available by alternative (non-classroom) means by 2001, rising to 50 per cent by 2003. This presents a considerable challenge for the MU EMEA staff. Content, delivery channels and support for learners all must be considered if the transfer away from classroom-based training is to be effective. Moreover, this transfer must take place in a global context: the key educational alliances with the univer-sity providers are determined in the USA. Extending technology-enabled learning throughout the world (with access for all employees) is considered critical to the company's business suc-cess. MU's motto is: 'Right knowledge, right now'.

In the words of Dr John O'Connor, the EMEA education tech-nology integrator:

> People in the telecommunications business need knowledge on several levels, including technical know-how, product-specific knowledge and competitive intelligence. Each of these requires a dynamic and evolving educational framework. The classroom model cannot efficiently deliver for large, disparate population groups. Motorolans need information that is relevant, up to date, on time and in manageable chunks. Learning technologies can play a strong part in making this scenario successful.

Production and delivery of content

The 30 per cent of training to be made available by non-classroom means embraces a number of technology-based approaches. It may include, for example, a synchronous (see page 115) satellite course broadcast from the USA. Many self-study courses are offered both through intranet (web) access and CD-ROM format. These materials are both generic (vendor-supplied) and internally customised to Motorola's needs as necessary. Subjects range from management and interpersonal skills to engineering.

Two innovations in learning technology are currently at an advanced stage. The first is an approach called Intranet Immediate Instruction (or I-cubed/I^3). This is a hardware/software solution that streams video images with audio, allowing subject matter experts within Motorola to produce one-off and regular messages or teaching modules. I-cubed is deployed within Motorola using a combination of tools that include Microsoft's 'MediaPlayer' viewer application. The education technology specialists have prepared both design and presenter guidelines to ensure that the final product is built on solid learning principles. MU has demonstrated that with well-designed storyboards and scripts, internal customers (worldwide) can access relevant, engaging messages or learning modules on the company intranet within 15 minutes of creation.

It is apparent that this solution type spans both communications and training – yet another illustration of the information-age phenomenon referred to as 'blur' (see page 12). In the first three months of I-cubed's operation, a series of diverse training modules have been developed and distributed. Topics include wireless access protocol (WAP) technology, product technical updates, performance review procedures and new employee induction.

The second innovation is the creation of a virtual reality (VR) PC-based solution laboratory for factory workers – designed to increase operational efficiency through off-line training. Using a matrix of digitised photographs, video and text/audio script within a VR modelling framework, the operation of an assembly machine can be simulated in all its operations. The intention is to make this training available adjacent to the production line in designated Motorola factories.

Learner support and learning centres

The nature of the business and its culture means that the company must expect Motorolans (their preferred term) to become receptive to technology-enabled learning. Most employees have PCs and for those who do not, or when geo-graphical constraints inhibit access to the intranet, the training can always be supplied on a CD-ROM. MU works with local learning representatives in many locations to assist with access or other problems.

In addition, MU has established learning centres at eight locations across the EMEA region. A typical learning centre has networked PCs with an administrator available to offer support. Other learning resources available at these facilities include books, videos, tapes, periodicals and language courses. Learning centres offer learning privacy in a supportive environment where people can get comfortable with PC-based learning.

> Learning centres may be thought of as a bridge between where we are in self-directed learning and where we'd like to be. If we were to build new learning areas, they might take the form of smaller kiosks nearer the workplace.

In John O'Connor's view, learning centres have historically focused on creating a broad resource library at the expense of the specific needs of learners. In some cases learning centres have been established without a strong business case (or indeed any business case at all). Realistically, these facilities need to be interwoven with the site-based business and performance needs to ensure that they do not evolve into wasteful or redundant 'landmarks'. Assuming the business need exists, constant mar-keting then becomes a key part of the success formula.

Motorola has been regarded as an early adopter of learning tech-nology and is confident of its future. E-learning will grow in importance as pressures on time intensify: 'Many people will look for five-minute learning interventions.'

However, MU is realistic about the limitations of technology-based approaches and the need to facilitate its acceptance. A recent 'Finance for Managers' training programme was designed to include a combination of CD-ROM training with 'live' coaching elements. Some users were confident with just content, others needed more face-to-face support from a finance 'coach', indicating different requirements for structure and social interaction with other learners. In John O'Connor's words, 'Go to the Web for definitions – go to the classroom for practice.'

The way of the future then is a balance between different forms of learning media. However, with technology-based methods increasing as a proportion of the total, more responsibility is placed on learners to plan, conduct and evaluate their own learning. John O'Connor describes the immediate e-learning future as 'self-directed within a disciplined framework'. More stringent milestones and a clearer support structure will need to be embedded if the full gains from new technology are to be realised.

My thanks to Dr O'Connor and Motorola University EMEA for their assistance in the preparation of this case study.

Case Study

BRITISH AIRWAYS QUEST AND COMMUNICATION POINTS

Introduction

For some time training professionals working for British Airways have been considering the issues involved in time and space to learn. They were offered a unique opportunity to implement a purpose design-solution when the company opened a new headquarters. The experience is outlined briefly below. British Airways would not claim to have solved the issues involved in time and space to learn, and is currently re-orienting and redesigning its approach. It is therefore particularly helpful of British Airways to share its experience.

Background

In 1997 British Airways moved its corporate headquarters to a new building – Waterside. Some 2,500 people would be located at this new purpose-built site. All would need access to training and to be able to participate in other communication activities built on new technologies.

Accordingly, in advance of the move, a series of technology trials were conducted. These examined how well training was received through the following delivery platforms: a discrete designated workstation in an office area; individual desktops using CD-ROMs; individual desktops via the LAN (local area network). These trials were designed to simulate full multimedia to the desktop in a low-technology environment. This allowed the identification and the preparation of a plan for the most appropriate method of delivery given the access to high-bandwidth technology in the new building. To quote from the report produced at the end of these trials:

> The preferred option for delivery is for a discrete workstation. Trialists reported that they were interrupted regularly when sitting at their own desk, as they were seen as accessible by colleagues. Telephones and e-mail were also a distraction to learning. The discrete area option was the preferred option for all the trialists, providing a more local learning environment considered better than the desk.

This 'discrete area option' had applications beyond training. There was a need to deliver other technology-led activities that could best be described as communications. Particularly important were those that used video, including desktop video conferencing, stored videos and British Airways TV (a service designed to give staff information on current matters as they affect the business).

The chosen solution was to establish 'QUEST and Communication Points'. 'QUEST' (an established internal brand) signalled that learning opportunities were available; 'communication' emphasised the other technologies.

Forty-five separate QUEST and communication points were installed at chosen locations in the Waterside building. Each contained a high specification PC that was branded to distinguish it from other desktop PCs. All could be used for applications by one or two people at the same time; all were connected to a fast transmission network; all were screened to ensure some privacy. Formally, the QUEST and communication points and network were corporately funded by the information management department. Due to copyright and licensing restriction, the programs were mainly limited to internally produced courses, though a number of IT training modules were available on licence.

Although the initiative produced some positive results, it was recognised that there was a need to increase the effectiveness and impact. In March 1999 a review was undertaken that showed that training was the most accessed resource at the points. The usage statistics highlighted the fact that the points were most used in the areas that had promoted their use and had requested additional coaching.

Julia Hilger-Ellis of the British Airways Training Team summed up the situation in the following terms: 'We will use the knowledge gained from the trials and implementation of the points to shape our future e-learning strategy.'

Generally, the following difficulties were identified. First, the QUEST and communication points were not always in the right locations. Second, there had been insufficient marketing. Third, the support required by some learners had not always been available at the time it was required. In addition, ownership and responsibility for the initiative was not sufficiently clear. Moreover, there had been uncertainty on purpose: the points had been introduced at the same time as a number of other changes following relocation to Waterside.

Currently, British Airways is relaunching the initiative, which will now be firmly owned by the training function. There will be a new marketing campaign, preceded by a consultation about location. There will also be a greater range of e-learning options made available through this platform. QUEST and communications points will, however, remain part of British Airways strategy.

My thanks to Julia Hilger-Ellis and the British Airways Training Team for their assistance in the preparation of this case study.

Chapter 6

The changing role
of the trainer

You've got to be careful if you don't know where you're going, because you might not get there

In the introduction to the book a target audience was identified as 'those involved in directing, managing or supporting the training function, irrespective of role or title'. The wider accountability for developing an organisation's human resource capital means that responsibility is far more dispersed.

This chapter is more specific in focus: it considers the role of the training manager or trainer in the organisation. Designations will vary – the word *learning* is starting to appear (mainly as a transatlantic import) in job titles, such as chief learning officer. However, we are talking about the roles and responsibilities of someone whose primary activities are designed to enhance the knowledge, skills and capabilities of individuals in the organisation. How will these roles be affected, what activities should be undertaken and what skills are required?

A starting point against which these perspectives can be reviewed is to return to the discussion on the new paradigm that form the conclusions of Chapter 3 (page 71). The contents of Focus Point 23 were tentatively proposed as the basis of that paradigm, which was described as learner-centred interventions. This will be the focus of the job of the training manager and trainers of the future.

Chapter 5 ended on a depressing note. The new technology, it was argued, offers training the opportunity to design and deliver interventions to suit the learners' needs. However, at this stage we simply do not know enough about how people learn in the new context.

Focus Point 23: Learner-centred interventions

A new paradigm will be based on learner-centred interventions. These will become a central accountability of the training manager and are characterised by:

📝 emphasis on the learners and their acceptance of their responsibility

📝 a holistic (or integrated) approach to creating competitive advantage through people in the organisation

📝 the need to ensure that resources are focused appropriately and managed effectively.

‘There are huge opportunities for increasing the job satisfaction of the individual trainer’

Fortunately, when we look at the changing role of the trainer in this chapter we can be much more positive. There are huge opportunities for enhancing the position of the profession and for increasing the job satisfaction of the individual trainer. The skill sets involved can be specified and identified and a start made.

These skills sets are summarised in the next proposition.

Proposition 16

Three distinct functional specialisms for trainers will evolve: design, delivery and learner support.

Some implications for these functional specialisms are developed in the course of this chapter. Two current perspectives on the role of the trainer are introduced as background. The first, which is drawn from some work undertaken in support of the promotion of National Vocational Qualifications (NVQs), is set out in Focus Point 24.

A second perspective makes a practical distinction. This is between the training professional (normally a training manager) who is

Focus Point 24: The trainer's role: a functional analysis

National Vocational Qualifications (NVQs) were originally introduced as a result of a UK government initiative launched in 1981;
they have been a central thrust of national training policy since
that date. The idea is that organisations are more likely to train
their employees (or employees will demand more training) if
there is a recognised system of qualifications in place that cover
all occupations. Moreover, those qualifications should be output-
based, and individuals should achieve them by demonstrating
competence against a set of agreed standards. Standards were set
by examining relevant jobs using a technique known as functional
analysis: a domain of work (for example, hairdressing) is identified; experts try to 'define' the activities undertaken in the field
of terms of outcomes; standards are set for these outcomes.

National Standards for Training and Development are now produced by the Employment National Training Organisation (see
www.empnto.co.uk/standards/training/index.htm). Previously they
were the responsibility of an organisation called the Training and
Development Lead Body. In 1995 a set of standards was developed that related to specified NVQ levels – including level 4 –
which demand competence in a broad range of complex, technical or professional work activities. A level 4 qualification was outlined as:

> aimed at those candidates who are involved in the delivery of
> learning programmes to individuals and groups. It requires candi-
> dates to identify the learning aims, needs and styles of individuals
> and to design and evaluate programmes to meet those individual
> requirements.[1]

The level 4 qualification was seen as more concerned with the
facilitation of a broader range of learning opportunities with
individuals and groups, rather than with direct instructional
training. To attain the qualification, candidates were required to
complete seven core units and five optional units. The core units
were:

- identify individuals' learning aims, needs and styles
- design learning programmes to meet learners' requirements
- create a climate conducive to learning

> ✐ agree learning programme with learners
> ✐ monitor and review progress with learners
> ✐ evaluate training and development programmes
> ✐ evaluate and develop own practice.
>
> There is much missing when considered against the job descrip-
> tion of many training managers: there is nothing about budgets,
> for example, or managing training through outsourced consult-
> ants. In fairness, however, the NVQ standards were not intended
> to be total job descriptions but to offer standards. Further, much
> of the management role was seen to be appropriate for the
> higher level 5 qualification.
>
> Nevertheless, the Learning Development NVQ is offered as a
> starting point because it is learner-focused. If the role of the
> training professional is to manage learner-centred interventions,
> the above list offers a good starting list of activities that should be
> undertaken.

working on the facilitation of a broader range of learning opportunities with individuals and groups, and those working on instructional development or delivery.

The distinction has been expressed thus:

> Acting as a strategic facilitator involves taking a clear managerial
> responsibility for the overall provision of training in the organization
> and its effectiveness – in particular a responsibility for the develop-
> ment of the training culture.

> In the alternative 'deliverer' role, the training professional does not
> assume primary management responsibility for the training effort;
> such responsibility lies elsewhere in the organization, with either the
> human resource function or line management, or a combination of
> both. Instead the training professional is relatively detached and he
> or she offers a specialized service of advice, design and delivery, with
> the aim of meeting needs identified by those responsible for the man-
> agement of the function.[2]

‘A new set of specialisms has emerged’

The potential gains from e-learning have increased the complexity and the focus of the role of the strategic facilitator (the training manager). As has been emphasised, that focus is now firmly on learner-centred interventions. The second role – 'specialised service of advice, design and delivery' (the trainer) – has also been dramatically altered: a new set of specialisms has emerged. Again the shorthand of 'training professional' will be used to encompass the training manager and the trainer.

Hard and soft technology

For both the strategic facilitator and the specialist trainer roles, the next proposition offers a useful starting point to consider the changes that follow from connectivity.

Proposition 17

A useful distinction can be made between hard technology and soft technology. The expertise of many trainers is in soft technology and this offers them an attractive future.

The concept of soft technology (and the distinction from hard technology) was introduced in Focus Point 16 in Chapter 5 (page 111). Hard technology refers to the information and communication technology systems and the architecture of these systems as applied to learning. They were illustrated in Figure 3 (page 45). Soft technology refers to those organisational activities that must be undertaken at all levels in an organisation to embed that hard technology effectively.

One of the recurrent themes throughout this book is that technology is an enabler. Proposition 4 (page 42), for example, states that there is a danger of being seduced by the functionality of the technology, rather than concentrating on its use. Proposition 12 (page 85) states that e-learning will be most effective for the acquisition of knowledge and least effective where interpersonal interaction is needed for learning. Proposition 13 (page 86) states that e-learning will be most effective as part of a systematic approach involving classroom and experiential learning with appropriate support.

Figure 15 develops the concept further by identifying the soft tech-nology components of a generalised e-learning system architecture. This figure is a parallel to the hard technology components set out in Figure 3. Together these figures can be of value in defining the issues that must be considered in implementing an e-learning solution.

The headings used in the bubbles reflect many of the issues discussed in the case studies that are introduced throughout the book. To follow the approach used in Chapter 2, where hard technology was considered (page 45), the following definitions may assist:

- *Promotion* – concerns the way that the system is marketed within the organisation. This extends beyond the production of leaflets and posters. It can also involve familiarisation training delivered to individuals at their desks.
- *Scope* – is about the applications of the learning system in the organisation. What is it designed to achieve? Is it, for example,

Figure 15
E-LEARNING SYSTEM ARCHITECTURE

Soft Technology

PROMOTION
Encouraging access and use

SCOPE
Targeting the use of the system

FIT
Defining relationship with other HR activity

INDIVIDUAL SUPPORT
Advising and assisting the learner in using the system

GROUP SUPPORT
Encouraging and facilitating the creation of learning communities

EVALUATION
Defining effectiveness of the learning system

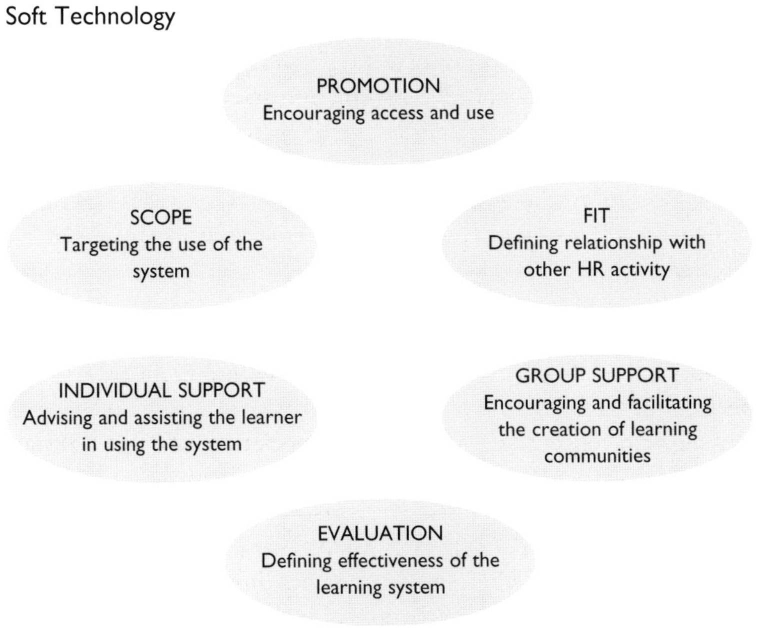

about getting learners to take more responsibility for their own development?

- ✍ *Fit* – is the way in which the learning system relates to other human resource activity, for example performance management or knowledge management.
- ✍ *Individual support* – extends beyond the initial familiarisation considered under 'Promotion' above. It embraces all of the on-going activity designed to help the learners take maximum advantage of the opportunities now available.
- ✍ *Group support* – is about the extent to which learning communities should be encouraged and supported. The term 'e-moderating' will be used for this activity later in the chapter.
- ✍ *Evaluation* – which scarcely needs an explanation – is a key feature of the trainer's role. The extent to which it has changed will be considered in a later section.

To emphasise: in e-learning, softer interventions that will be delivered by a skilled individual will always be important.

A well-rehearsed parody in the business world illustrates the continued role of the softer interventions. It goes as follows: e-business will be overtaken by m-business, which depends on information delivered through wireless technology (mobile phones). In turn, however, this will be superseded by s-business – which will make rapid advances, particularly in retail.

An s-business approach to purchasing clothes, for example, involves the following activities: an individual would enter a physical outlet and be presented with a range of alternatives; he or she would be able to try them on for size and get an immediate appreciation of colours; other s-business outlets could be visited. These s-business outlets would be branded as 'shops' and would offer a high-touch alternative to the high-tech approach of e-business. Venture capitalists are optimistic that the s-business model will succeed!

Getting the right balance between high-tech (delivery through systems) and high touch (delivery through personal interaction) is recognised as a key element in all aspects of business activity in the connected economy. Figure 16 is taken from an internal Ernst & Young illustration that outlines the changing pattern of e-business

Figure 16
E-BUSINESS CASE – PROFESSIONAL SERVICES

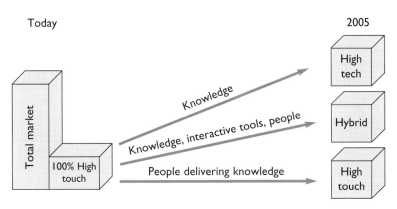

Reproduced with permission of Ernst & Young

in professional services. Today a small proportion of the total market is exclusively high touch. In the future the model will be more fragmented (or blurred!): some knowledge will be delivered using high-tech means; people will also be required to deliver knowledge using high touch; there will be hybrid solutions (involving both technology and personal interventions) in between. This model will apply to training; the parallels are exact. The skills required of the professional will reflect the delivery requirements of the model.

The changing skills: an ASTD view

In 1998 the American Society for Training and Development published the results of an important study. This concerned a wide-ranging review of the challenge that the influx of learning development technologies posed for HR professionals. To quote:

> The ability to decide on and use an emerging array of learning technologies in a variety of roles is rapidly becoming a key set of required competencies for HRD professionals. Whether the HRD function is training, human performance improvement, or something else, it is increasingly evident that HRD departments must have staff members who are capable of using learning technologies for training and development. These capabilities ensure that the department can perform tasks ranging from advising on technology systems acquisition to designing and using specific technology applications to providing

the logistical support often required for technology-based delivery. The training team must play a role in all of these activities, as well as in the design, development, and delivery of training using whatever technology mix is appropriate.[3] (p26)

The ASTD study identified eight distinct roles in the implementation of e-learning. These are reproduced in Focus Point 25. To an extent they can be mapped to the roles that have been discussed earlier in this chapter.

The first two roles (HRD manager and analyst) relate to activities undertaken by strategic facilitators. This also applies to the evaluator role, though mastery of this activity is critical to all training professionals. The other ASTD roles can be clustered around the specialisms involved in Proposition 16 (three distinct functional specialisms for trainers will evolve: design, delivery and learner support). 'Design' embraces the ASTD's designer and developer roles. 'Delivery' embraces both implementation and instructor. The ASTD's eighth role of organisational change agent embraces learning support, the third specialism in the key proposition. However, the correspondence is far less exact. An important point is at issue here.

Generally the US literature is far less advanced in the softer areas of learner support. There is a real opportunity for trainers in Europe to contribute to thinking and practice on this topic; there is a strong tradition of soft-skill intervention which can offer a solid foundation for development.

Design and delivery

Where the US literature and practice is strong is on the harder skills of instructional systems development (ISD). This term was introduced in Chapter 3, and Figure 5 reproduces a table taken from the same ASTD report that considered the new roles for trainers outlined immediately above.

There is a rich and continuing US discipline of applying sound instructional principles to training. As long ago as 1946, the US educator and writer Edgar Dale introduced the 'cone of experience'. This has found its way into countless 'train the trainers' sessions. In crude

Focus Point 25: Roles for learning technologies –
the ASTD analysis

Role	Description of the role
HRD manager	Determines which learning technology, or combination of technologies, an organisation should use to meet the comprehensive needs of the company. Decides when these technologies should be used and monitors the progress of all the other roles in the delivery process.
Analyst	Identifies performance gaps and recommends performance objectives that address the gaps. Determines if training is the proper intervention.
Designer	Determines what content, instructional methods, presentation methods and distribution methods will achieve the desired objectives and will suit the needs of the trainee population. Also creates the design document that will integrate all of these elements.
Developer	Uses the design document to create materials that are delivered via various presentation methods.
Implementor	Works with technical staff to set up and provide logistical support for technology devices. Also works with suppliers to produce and distribute electronic training materials.
Instructor	Facilitates learning either in a live broadcast or in an advanced technology classroom.
Evaluator	Measures the success of the source objectives and the effectiveness of the technology.
Organisational change agent	Helps the organization adapt to the new technology and see its value and benefits.

Reproduced with permission from the American Society for Training and Development.[3]

summary, it states that people generally remember: 10 per cent of what they read; 20 per cent of what they hear; 30 per cent of what they see; 50 per cent of what they hear and see; 70 per cent of what they say and write; 90 per cent of what they say as they do a thing.

The ISD approach has been given new impetus as the technology available has become more sophisticated. Using a systems processing approach provides the basis of a framework that leads to practical implementation.

To quote from the author and consultant Deborah Schreiber:

> Distance and distributed education and training represent a process composed of multiple and diverse elements. These elements or components are associated with several categories, including the learner, instructor, learning environment, instructional delivery technology, and the culture of the organization providing the training.
>
> Applying the systems processing approach of ISD to the development and delivery of distance and distributed training provides a strategy for understanding the roles of the student located at a remote site and the instructor designing materials to be delivered at a distance over some technical medium. A systems processing strategy enables investigation of the relationships amongst the various elements of the process, including, in addition to the student and instructor, the learning environment (for example, site planning for a satellite broadcast, or desktop access), the instructional technology (compressed video or Internet), and the culture of the institution or agency (including level of organizational technology capability for providing distance training).[4] (p39)

For any training professional with an ambition to specialise in e-learning design, the message is simple. First, investigate the US literature. Two books are recommended: one is *Distance Training* by Schreiber and Berge, from which the above quotation is taken; the second book is *The ASTD Handbook of Training Design and Delivery*.[5] Regular articles and discussions also appear in the ASTD's magazine *Training and Development*. A valuable UK volume is Judith Christian-Carter's *Mastering Instructional Design in TBT*.[6] For those who wish to acquire a real specialism, it will be increasingly possible in this age of blur to acquire a distance qualification in instructional system development from a reputable US university.

Two final points should be made on design and delivery in e-learning. The first concerns design for the Web and the second the other skills of delivery.

Given the current growth of e-business, effective web design has, of course, become a hot topic. Much of the current debate is focused on the business-to-consumer (B2C) sites and business-to-business (B2B) sites. Learning systems that concern business-to-employee (B2E) interface have not received the same attention. Nevertheless, the same principles apply and a set of best practice rules are emerging. It seems sensible to accept, for example, that a user's main concern is getting access to the information immediately. A standard sequence, therefore, would be first to decide on content and then to work out navigation. For those wishing to pursue this aspect of design further, the work of Jakob Nielsen is recommended. He has researched and written extensively on the Web and usability: his recent book is called *Designing Web Usability*[7] and his website is www.useit.com.

The point to be made on the other skills of delivery is straightforward. Proposition 13 (page 86) argues that e-learning will be most effective as part of a systematic approach involving classroom and experiential learning with appropriate support. The traditional skills of the trainer must never be overlooked – even if they are delivered in a different context.

Supporting learners: digital collaboration

As should be apparent from the arguments advanced in recent sections of this book, developing effective learner support may be the major challenge facing the training profession. The connected economy allows learner-centred interventions to be designed and delivered; this will require support for individual learners across a range of activities. As was suggested in the previous chapter, the topic is under-researched. The USA has a strong tradition of instructional systems development but is less advanced in this softer area.

‘ Developing effective learner
support may be the major
challenge ’

However, what can be stated with confidence is that there is a body of knowledge on discrete activities (or elements) involved in learner support. Taken together with a more effective research base, they could amount to a new discipline. Certainly there are opportunities for individual trainers to identify and acquire the new skill set.

Broadly, these skills can be divided into two: those that are related immediately to the delivery of training using technology and those that take place independently of any e-learning activity. This second category is the more traditional role, which is well developed in the literature.

The work of Elliott Masie, whose publications have already been cited throughout this book, offers much guidance on the first category. He uses the term digital collaboration to describe the situation where:

> two or more people [are] working or learning together, separated by distance and perhaps time.
>
> Digital collaboration will turn our desktops, laptops, cell phones and handheld/wearable devices into rich media communicators. Our corporate networks will increasingly be used for collaboration and communication, as well as transactions and content delivery.[8]

Providing support for learners participating in digital collaboration involves a range of activities. These include support for access to technology, pre-learning activities and post-learning reinforcement. One aspect where there is a developing literature is the moderation or facilitation of online discussion groups. Much of the experience that has been gained to date has arisen in an educational context. Significant expertise has been developed as a result of interventions designed to enhance learner experience in universities using modern distance-learning techniques – both in the UK and overseas. This is outlined in the next section.

Supporting learners – e-moderating

Gilly Salmon, a senior lecturer at the Open University Business School, has offered a most useful practical contribution in her book *E-Moderating: The key to teaching and learning online*.[9] Most helpfully, and in the spirit of knowledge-sharing, she has established an e-moderating homepage at http://oubs.open.ac.uk/e-moderating.

Salmon describes the e-moderator as someone who presides over an electronic meeting or conference. Such an activity demands a different awareness and approach from a face-to-face meeting and requires a rather wider range of expertise.

Her preferred term to describe much of the activity is computer-mediated conferencing (CMC).

> CMC provides a way of sending messages to a group of users, using computers for storage and mediation. A computer, somewhere, holds all the messages until a participant is ready to log on and access them, so on-line conferences do not require participants to be available at a particular time.[9] (pp15–16) [This is a form of asynchronous activity – see Focus Point 18, page 115.]

Three types of technology are involved: a server and software system, a terminal or personal computer for each user and a telecommunications system to connect the computers to the server. This hard technology will doubtless increase dramatically in functionality. The introduction of video clips showing the individual talking is an obvious development. The soft technology requires skills and management.

In her book and associated website, Gilly Salmon presents a five-stage model drawn from her research. The broad headings of these stages are: access and motivation; online socialisation; information exchange; knowledge construction; and development. If these stages progress effectively, a community in which individuals gain and share knowledge can be built. The tasks of the e-moderator vary and evolve at each stage (from welcoming and encouraging at the first stage, for example, to supporting and responding at the last). A set of online competencies for e-moderators are developed from this analysis and presented and explored in her book.

Computer-mediated conferencing may manifest itself differently in the corporate environment from in the academic. Online communities may, for example, have a shorter life expectancy in the corporate environment (they may be focused on a particular project); the

motivation of participants may be different. However, the importance of effective moderation will remain an issue and there is much
to be learned.

Consider the following comments from Professor David Asch, who par-
ticipated in a group that bridged a corporate and academic community.

> First some general observations. There are a limited number of con-
> tributors in each of the sections; the discussion leaders of each seem
> to be trying hard to engage individuals in the debate; of course I do
> not know how many of the others are 'lurking' and not contributing
> (as I was). Second, after an initial flurry of activity little seems to be
> happening. I suspect this is because of a lack of focus, or perhaps a
> lack of interest, or maybe because people involved find that the 'dis-
> cussions' appear to lack structure and direction.

> I must admit to finding the discussions (of potentially very interest-
> ing topics) somewhat uninspiring. I do not know how the groups
> were set up or what they were supposed to do. But on the basis of
> what I've read, and the quality of that, it did appear that more focus
> and direction would have helped to lift the level of debate and hence
> to engage more people if they could see some benefit for themselves
> from involvement. I would suspect that given the nature of the
> people, the importance of the topic and the importance of learning
> that the process may have been facilitated by being somewhat more
> directive not only in terms of content and development of outcomes,
> but perhaps more importantly in terms of process and timescales.

Managing learner-centred intervention is a new discipline. However,
jobs are emerging and Focus Point 26 is a reproduction of the first
UK job description of one of the new roles. This is set out in a summary of an e-moderating job at **learndirect** – the brand name for the
University for Industry (Ufi). This government-supported initiative
forms a case study included at the end of Chapter 8 (page 192).

Supporting learners

Earlier in this chapter it was emphasised that the traditional skills of
the trainer must never be overlooked. The ability to deliver material
to an audience, to manage interaction in the classroom and to build
the learner's self-confidence on a one-to-one basis remain key skills
of value to the organisation. The arrival of e-learning simply means
that they will be delivered in a new context.

Focus Point 26: E-moderating: learndirect job outlines

The job

Reporting to the e-learning manager, you will have responsibility for the delivery of high-quality learner support of a non-subject-specific nature. You will be instrumentally involved in determining reasonable learner support requirements and will work closely with your e-learning facilitator colleagues to provide support to match these requirements. You will provide much of this support synchronously within the learndirect online working environment. You will need to work flexibly, at various times of the day and not necessarily to uniform work patterns. Your role will involve some evening and weekend work.

Prime responsibilities

1   Implement Ufi's innovative learner support model, both nationally and throughout the hub network.
2   Proactively support online learners who require motivating and who are experiencing simple problems.
3   Signpost learners to other services providing in-depth support or advice.
4   Work with the team to implement and update databases of frequently asked questions (FAQs).
5   Facilitate national learner conferences within the Ufi website to encourage and develop usage of the support services.
6   Support online tutors and facilitators from Ufi hubs using the online tutor conference.
7   Train online tutors and facilitators as necessary.
8   Administer the online tools.
9   Develop and implement ideas for the dynamic learning website with other members of the distributed learning team.
10   Help in developing Ufi standards for learner support.
11   Monitor the application of Ufi standards for learner support.
12   Identify and share good practice in learner support.

Qualifications, skills and experience
Essential

1   Educated to degree level or equivalent.
2   Minimum of two years' experience of face-to-face tutoring and facilitation or other learning support role.

3   Sound understanding of the differences between online and face-to-face tutoring.
4   Highly developed interpersonal skills.
5   Experience of using common computer applications and e-mail.
6   Experience in planning, developing and organising training.
7   Proven ability to contribute as a team member to group outcomes.

Reproduced with thanks to the University for Industry (Ufi).

One of the bullet points used to clarify the concept of learner-centred interventions in Focus Point 23 was 'emphasis on the learners and their acceptance of their responsibility'. A whole series of approaches, techniques or mechanisms has been developed to assist in this process. All fall into the broad category of softer interventions. There is much literature available on these approaches.

Some illustrations, taken from current practice at Ernst & Young, may assist.[10]

The first concerns the clarification of some of the processes involved in one-to-one learning support. Focus Point 27 offers a set of definitions.

The second illustration concerns one approach used in group support: the encouragement of self-managed learning groups. Focus Point 28 outlines the proposition used at Ernst & Young to facilitate the establishment of such groups. The underlying process is set out in Figure 17.

‘e-learning allows training interventions to be made much more transparent for the learner’

Additionally one obvious advantage of e-learning is that it allows training interventions to be made much more transparent for the

Focus Point 27: The helping process: some definitions

Coaching, counselling and mentoring are all regarded as 'helping processes', and all can assist in accelerating the learning and performance of staff. They are defined as follows:

- *Coaching* – a process in which a manager, through direct discussion and guided activity, helps a colleague to solve a problem or a task more effectively than would otherwise have been the case. It also includes the process of producing personal development and action plans. Coaching is task-centred in that it focuses upon the work processes, appropriate behaviours and the actions the individual needs to take to improve performance.
- *Counselling* – a process that helps the individual resolve personal issues that impede effective work performance or the development of new skills and attitudes. The style of delivery is usually non-directive/neutral. Counselling is person-centred in that it focuses upon whatever the issues may be for an individual.
- *Mentoring* – a process that helps a person handle significant transitions in responsibility and/or status. It provides advice on such issues as the suitability of career goals, personal strategies and tactics. There will normally be a significant difference in seniority between mentors and those assisted.

learner. These interventions can be promoted as learning systems (not to be confused with the narrow use of the term – as a vendor's product – in Chapter 2). An illustrative learning system, for senior Ernst & Young staff who are aiming for partnership, is set out as Figure 18.

Irrespective of the approach used, providing effective learner support will be a critical professional accountability for the future. Opportunities are evident in instructional design and development. What this chapter should hopefully have demonstrated is the wide range and scope that e-learning has created for trainers. If we fail to take advantage, we will have no one to blame but ourselves.

> ### Focus Point 28: Self-managed learning groups
>
> A self-managed learning group brings together a number of people with a similar broad objective (for example, partnership entry). With the assistance of a coaching specialist they form a group, develop an agenda and decide how to organise themselves going forward.
>
> The objectives of such a group for the individual are defined as follows:
>
> - enables you to produce a tailored programme – learning goals, strategies, methods, tactics – to suit you
> - helps you maintain momentum: challenges, reviews your progress, provides feedback
> - raises self-awareness
> - provides useful content – but not a talking shop!
>
> The added-value outcomes are finding out:
>
> - how to learn from experience
> - how to operate in ambiguous situations
> - how to measure your progress
> - how to develop your career.
>
> The principles of operation are to:
>
> - show interest in others
> - be open to others
> - be open with others
> - expect achievement
> - assess achievement
> - expect agreements to be kept
> - challenge yourself and others.

References

1   See *Standards in Training and Development: A summary of the framework and qualification structure.* London, Department of Employment, 1998. The units cited are taken from N/SVQ Level 4: Learning Development.

2   SLOMAN M. *A Handbook for Training Strategy.* 2nd edn. Aldershot, Gower, 1999. p233.

Figure 17
SELF-MANAGED LEARNING

The process

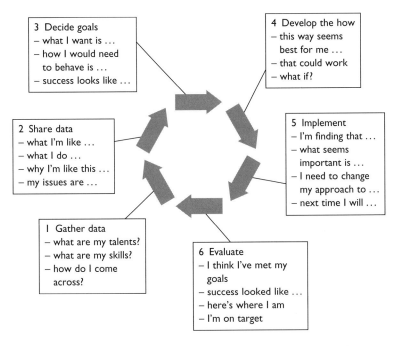

3   PISKURICH G. M. *and* SANDERS E. S. *ASTD Models for Learning Technologies: Roles, competencies and outputs.* Alexandria, Va., American Society of Training and Development, 1998.

4   SCHREIBER D. A. *and* BERGE Z. L. (EDS) *Distance Training.* San Francisco, Jossey-Bass, 1998.

5   PISKURICH G. M., BECKSCHI P. *and* HALL B. *The ASTD Handbook of Training Design and Delivery.* New York, McGraw-Hill, 2000.

6   CHRISTIAN-CARTER J. *Mastering Instructional Design in TBT.* London, Chartered Institute of Personnel and Development, 2001.

7   NEILSEN J. *Designing Web Usability.* Indianapolis, New Riders, 2000.

8   MASIE E. 'Digital collaboration: the next wave of corporate technology'. *Learning Decisions.* June 2000.

Figure 18
CORE LEARNING SYSTEM FOR PARTNER TRACK

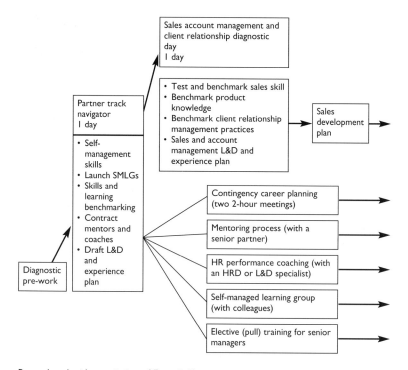

Reproduced with permission of Ernst & Young

9   SALMON G. *E-Moderating: The key to teaching and learning online.* London, Kogan Page, 2000.

10 I am grateful to my colleagues Des Woods and Mike Laws for permission to reproduce their work.

Chapter 7

Training in
transition

When asked by a waitress whether he wanted his pizza cut into four or eight pieces: *Better make it four – I don't think I can eat eight*

Changes caused by connectivity will be far-reaching. The whole training industry could be altered, and it is difficult to predict what steady state will be attained. At the heart of this lies the economic forces that were discussed in Chapter 1. These are summarised in Focus Point 29.

The previous chapter looked at the way the skill set of trainers will change. The implication throughout was that they would be working in a corporate role or offering bought-in services as a consultant. Inspection of the ASTD analysis of roles set out in Focus Point 25 (page 147) shows that many of these functions could be delivered from either of these standpoints.

This chapter widens the analysis beyond the role of the individual. It considers the potential implications for the training industry as a whole by illustrating the power of changing market relationships. It then focuses on strategic resource management – re-emphasising the importance of effective evaluation.

Changing market relationships

Focus Point 29 contains a generic list of components of the new business model that will emerge as a result of connectivity. All could apply, to a greater or lesser degree, to the training industry. Indeed, a lot of activities reflecting these forces have already been put in place. Some initiatives have proved successful; some less successful; with some it is too early to tell. What is beyond doubt is that the traditional boundaries and relationships between suppliers could disappear or be blurred. Two illustrations from the USA may assist.

Focus Point 29: Key components of new business models

- low-cost access to global markets/suppliers
- reduced marketing and sales costs for businesses
- 24-hour shopping and reduced costs for customers
- elimination of traditional intermediaries and emerging new intermediaries
- further/cheaper connections between businesses, leading to reduced costs and increased agility in the supply chain
- enhanced communication with internal stakeholders leading to faster responses and improved speed to market
- new entrants into markets supplying completely new offerings, potentially eliminating existing players in that market.

Reproduced by permission of Ernst & Young

One early initiative was the establishment in 1995 in the USA of the executive education network. This involved a consortium of leading business schools (including Wharton, Penn State and Babson) and a specialist communications company. The aim was to offer high-quality business school teaching to corporate clients. Managers assembled in classrooms, received synchronous classroom tuition via satellite and were supported by local tutors or business school specialists.

Despite its superficial attractions – top-quality business education delivered locally – the initiative did not develop. According to some of the business school staff involved, there were late cancellations and substitutions: too many participants did not undertake their pre-reading. Moreover, those participants who received the teaching by satellite felt at a disadvantage compared with those who were located with the lead tutor. The tutors in the satellite classrooms were often untrained or simply absent.[1]

‘It would be a brave second-division business school who would invest in a product that competes directly with Harvard’

The second illustration concerns the current initiatives under way at Harvard Business School. Harvard has a powerful reputation and hence an immensely strong brand. To many, the key to Harvard's success is the reputation of its faculty, the quality and practical relevance of its research and its ability to teach using the case study method. Its executive education courses can therefore command a considerable premium. In summer 2000 Harvard Business School Publishing launched High Performance Management On-Line. This is an intranet/Internet tool using multimedia technology offering interactive case studies. A number of *Harvard Business Review* articles are built in as a resource library. The 20 topic areas include exercising power and influence, managing change, and even the softer skills of coping with stress and emotion. Does this initiative dilute Harvard's brand, or is it leveraging its competitive advantage into a new market? Time will tell. What is important in the context of this discussion is a recognition that one of the most senior players in executive education is prepared to compete in a different way. Given the global reach of the Internet, it would be a brave second-division business school who would invest in a product that competes directly with Harvard.

These illustrations show how connectivity will affect the training market. It will be some time before the impact of current initiatives will become apparent. However, for the longer term, the next proposition can be advanced with confidence.

Proposition 18

Any part of the training supply chain that does not add value will disappear. Other parts could well become commodity products.

The concept of a supply or value chain for training was outlined in Chapter 4 (pages 81–82). The outline value chain presented there is reproduced as Figure 19. In Chapter 4 it was argued that those responsible for training should consider the chain that applies in their organisation. In the context of this chapter it should be recognised that each of the players in the training industry must consider the value that they add. To survive they must understand that the market is changing and that transparency of information will drive down costs.

Figure 19
THE SUPPLY OR VALUE CHAIN

A generic model

How it might appear to the training manager

What is the training content – the building blocks of knowledge and skill elements? Who creates or supplies them?	How are the building blocks put together into a cohesive module or programme? Is this done in-house or outsourced?	How are the modules or programmes delivered? Are they courses, technology-based training or experiential events?	How are the end users made aware of the events? How do they access them?	What support does the end user (the learner) need and how is it delivered? What is the reinforcement of learning (the after-sales service)?

Raw Materials $\rightarrow$ Manufacturing $\rightarrow$ Distribution $\rightarrow$ Marketing $\rightarrow$ Customer

Consider, for example, the first column in Figure 19, the provision of raw material or content. Here, as has been noted, Harvard has recently made a significant intervention in the market. More generally, despite an overall attempt to create a mystique, most of the soft skills training elements are straightforward: the tools and techniques used in, say, performance feedback, interviewing skills or facilitation do not vary a great deal from trainer to trainer. One of the standard pieces of business guidance in coping with the changes brought about by connectivity is 'give your product away free: make your money through services'. Basic training content could, on this basis, become a commodity. The premium is to be gained from effective customisation or delivery – especially in the classroom. Put another way, for the smaller training consultancy the future may lie in high touch (one-to-one or group delivery) rather than high technology.

This obviously poses a tremendous challenge for all external training consultants. The two case studies set out at the end of this chapter show how two very different organisations – MDA and Dove Nest – are exploring the current opportunities.

Changing relationships across the supply or value chain will give rise to a whole range of problems. Many of these are still to emerge, but one that can be firmly identified concerns copyright and access. If the basic 'knowledge' components are made available over the intranet

> **Focus Point 30: Extract from Ernst & Young invitation to tender**
>
> 10   Intellectual property
>
> The successful bidder must confirm acceptance of Section 10.1, 10.2, and 10.3.
>
> 10.1 Any Ernst & Young models, single frames, tools etc shared with the successful bidder must not be disclosed to a third party.
>
> 10.2 Any general models, outlines on training approaches (such as could be placed on the intranet) will remain the property of Ernst & Young.
>
> 10.3 Any specific classroom materials will remain the property of the training consultant, but will be made available to Ernst & Young to be used outside the UK, at an agreed fee.

(and also used in the classroom), who will own the intellectual property? Once again it is the business and commercial drivers that will determine the agenda. The current formulation used in Ernst & Young's invitation to tender is set out in Focus Point 30. It may assist corporate organisations who use outsourced training organisations as the main means of delivery.

Strategic resource management

Irrespective of the changing relationships across the value chain, resource allocation will remain an issue of key importance. The collection and analysis of effective economic measures (or metrics) will remain an essential role for the training function. For example, Elliott Masie has offered the following formats for expressing e-learning budget figures.

> Cost per new hire for stage one training; Cost per virtual course; Cost per employee for infrastructure; Cost per product release; Cost per year for learning management service. These are just a few of the metrics that we see popping up in the budget section of strategies.[2]

The objective of effective deployment of resources is not altered by the introduction of e-learning. However, as the next proposition suggests, the focus may shift.

Proposition 19

Time, not spend, will become a scarce resource. Monitoring of use and evaluation of effectiveness will become critically important.

The phrase 'work-intensive' is often used to characterise modern society. For many people work is interesting, fulfilling, demanding but exhausting: there is always something else of value to do.

Proposition 19 should not be taken to suggest that expenditure on training no longer matters. Appropriate financial disciplines must apply to day-to-day budgetary control; investment decisions (increasingly concerned with the purchase of technology-based systems) must be subjected to the appropriate rigorous analysis. What the proposition does is draw a further inference from the new paradigm that formed the conclusion of Chapter 3 – the move to learner-centred interventions.

‹ Time for individual learning competes with other organisational demands ›

If the focus is shifted to learners, and efforts concentrated on ways to make them acquire skills and knowledge in the most efficient way, their time becomes the scarce resource. Time for individual learning competes with other organisational demands: time for client contact and selling, creative time to develop new products, time to develop staff, time for general administration. Increasingly there is a challenge to excessive organisational demands competing with personal and domestic needs. There is a demand for an appropriate work–life balance. The ability of the connected economy to deliver training material to the learner 'any time, any place' poses an obvious danger of a further intrusion into personal space ('I'll try and fit it in over the weekend').

Since for the learner time is the critical resource, so, in accordance with the new paradigm, it must become for the organisation. Time must become a focus of evaluation interventions. Here the new connectivity offers a huge benefit: one element in many e-learning systems is behaviour and usage analysis. This is the ability to automatically generate information on how much any individual uses a system. In short, learner-centred measurement becomes feasible. In the author's experience at Ernst & Young, this ability to monitor usage was considered by senior management to be of considerable benefit. Focus Point 31 discusses how the concept of clickstream data could be used to assist the effectiveness of training.

This learner-centred measurement should be placed in the overall framework of training evaluation.

The most common evaluation framework adopted by training practitioners in the USA, the Kirkpatrick model, offers four levels of evaluation:

✎ *Reaction* – how well did training participants like the programme?
✎ *Learning* – what knowledge (principles, facts and techniques) did participants gain from the programme?
✎ *Behaviour* – what positive changes in participants' job behaviour stemmed from the training programme?
✎ *Results* – what were the training programme's organisational effects in terms of reduced costs, improved quality of work, increased quantity of work and so forth?[3]

Kirkpatrick, then, suggests that evaluation can be implemented at a series of different levels. An important gain from technology is that participant responses are easy to collect electronically. This requires the design and implementation of appropriate systems. Focus Point 32 contains a suite of participant feedback forms for web-based courses designed for use in Ernst & Young courses in the USA.[4] Examination of these forms indicates that they do generate some information on higher-level evaluation, but here much of the feedback should also be collected by questionnaire-based interview. For an outline of this approach see the section in the author's previous work.[5]

Focus Point 31: Clickstream data

When people explore a website, their mouse clicks generate data that reflect their behaviour. This information is called clickstream data. Proposition 2 (page 7) argued that the drivers of Internet activity and development are business and commercial. These will shape and foreshadow developments in training. This proposition applies to the importance of clickstream data. Commercial organisations are using the data to learn how to design sites, how to make them user-friendly, how to market them and how to personalise pages.

Commercial data that could be tracked typically includes the following items:

- Where did a visitor first land on a site?
- What attracted them to the site?
- How many pages were viewed and in what order?
- How long did the visitor spend on each site?

For the commercial Internet company, the potential value of such clickstream data is evident. It can be used to determine advertising strategy. It can also be used to influence site design. The latter is most immediately analogous to the requirements of effective training. The aim is to attract learners to sites, make it easy to navigate and thus promote efficient learning.

A whole collection of packages have been developed to assist with clickstream analysis for business Internet sites. Similar packages will doubtless be developed as learning systems become more popular. The issue facing those responsible for training will then be to determine what specific information will be of value to improve the opportunities for the learner.

Before this discussion on resource management concludes, one other difference that could result from e-learning should be noted. This concerns user reaction to a poor training experience. An important distinction is that an adverse reaction to course-based training can lead to complaints; an adverse reaction to e-learning can lead to embarrassment. If someone has spent three days on a course (remember, time is the scarce resource) that was perceived to be a waste of time, they may well articulate their reaction forcefully. The training

Focus Point 32: Participant feedback form

Please mark the box that best describes your level of satisfaction using the scale below

5	4	3	2	1	N/A
Strongly agree	**Agree**	**Neither agree nor disagree**	**Disagree**	**Strongly disagree**	**Not applicable**

LEARNING EFFECTIVENESS

1 I clearly understood the course objectives.   5 4 3 2 1 N/A

2 The course objectives were relevant to my   5 4 3 2 1 N/A
   needs.

3 The course was appropriate for me, given   5 4 3 2 1 N/A
   my knowledge and experience.

4 The knowledge and/or skills gained through   5 4 3 2 1 N/A
   this course are directly applicable to my job.

5 Overall, this course was an effective   5 4 3 2 1 N/A
   learning experience.

6 List what you liked best about this learning
   experience.

   _____

   _____

   _____

   _____

   _____

After completing this programme, I am confident that I can meet the following objectives...
(The following examples are objectives from Supply Chain 101)

1 Articulate key leading practices in supply   5 4 3 2 1 N/A
   chain management.

2 Identify supply chain metrics and value   5 4 3 2 1 N/A
   propositions.

3 Assist in the completion of a supply chain   5 4 3 2 1 N/A
   current state assessment.

4   Mine for knowledge and learn how to find   5 4 3 2 1 N/A
     resources (eg the supply chain powerpack)
     that can assist in the support supply chain
     engagements.

COURSE DESIGN

1   The course content was logically organised.   5 4 3 2 1 N/A

2   The course content was clearly written.   5 4 3 2 1 N/A

3   The use of audio enhanced my learning   5 4 3 2 1 N/A
     experience.

4   The course activities reinforced the content. 5 4 3 2 1 N/A

5   The length of this course was ...
                    ☐ Too long   ☐ Just right   ☐ Too short

COURSE DELIVERY

1   I was able to access this course when I   5 4 3 2 1 N/A
     needed it.

2   The delivery method(s) used in this course   5 4 3 2 1 N/A
     was an effective way for me to learn the
     subject matter.

3   The amount of time it took me to access   5 4 3 2 1 N/A
     this course was acceptable.

4   It was easy to navigate through the web-   5 4 3 2 1 N/A
     based learning product to find the
     information I needed.

5   These features were helpful and informative.

     a) Help   5 4 3 2 1 N/A
     b) Site map   5 4 3 2 1 N/A
     c) Progress report   5 4 3 2 1 N/A
     e) Other (please list)   5 4 3 2 1 N/A

6   The setting in which I took this course was a(n):
     (Check appropriate box)

     a) office   ☐
     b) hotel   ☐
     c) client's   ☐

d) home   ☐
e) other (please specify)   ☐

7   The setting (eg office, hotel, client's, home)   5 4 3 2 1 N/A
    in which I took this course was appropriate.

ANTICIPATED IMPACT

Questions 1 and 2 require that you express your answer in increments of 10%.

1   What percentage of your total working time do you or will
    you spend on tasks that require the skills/knowledge
    presented in this course?   _____ %

2   Considering your work tasks, what percentage of the
    knowledge/skills presented in this programme did you have
    a working knowledge of ...

    a) before this course?   _____ %
    b) after this course?   _____ %

3   List two to three tasks, activities or responsibilities to which
    you plan to apply the skills and knowledge you gained from
    this course:

    a) _____
    b) _____
    c) _____

4   List ways in which your job performance will improve as a
    result of taking this course.

    a) _____
    b) _____
    c) _____

OPPORTUNITY FOR IMPROVEMENTS

1   List any barriers that may prevent you from using the
    knowledge and skills gained from this course.

    _____
    _____
    _____

2   List any enablers that would help you use the knowledge
    and skills you gained from this course more effectively.

    _____

    _____

    _____

3   List what you liked least about this course.

    _____

    _____

    _____

4   List any changes in content, delivery, formatting, etc that
    would improve this course.

    _____

    _____

    _____

manager/human resource manager can expect a strongly worded e-mail or telephone conversation.

At present, and this could pass, an adverse reaction to Internet/intranet training may be conveniently forgotten. Assume the learner is expected to access a module at his or her convenience (asynchronous training, see page 115). If the experience is unfavourable (because of difficult access, bad navigation or inappropriate content, for example), the module will not be revisited. Certainly in the current climate the learner may well lack the confidence to complain. It is in all parties' interests – the trainer's and the learner's – to say nothing at the time.

Effective learner support is needed to try to ensure that this problem does not arise or that it is dealt with effectively after the event.

This chapter has focused on the economic forces affecting the training industry; the previous chapter focused on the role of the individual. The conclusions from both are positive: the prospects for capable individuals and quality consultancies are good. We all have reason to be optimistic. For those who are positive, embrace change and can learn new skills, an exciting future beckons. The starting point is to ask 'Where can I add value?' As Aristotle is reported to have said:

> Where your talents and the needs of the world cross, there lies your vocation.

References

1   BYRNE J. A. 'Virtual b-schools'. *Business Week*. October 23, 1995. pp64–8. My thanks to my friends at Penn State, especially Al Vicere, for the additional insights.

2   From *Learning Decisions*. September 2000.

3   KIRKPATRICK D. L. *Evaluating Training Programs*. Alexandria, Va., American Society for Training and Development, 1975.

4   I am grateful to Bob Blondin and Bill Diffley of the US practice of Ernst & Young for their permission to reproduce these questionnaires.

5   SLOMAN M. *A Handbook for Training Strategy*. 2nd edn. Aldershot, Gower, 1999. pp194–9.

Case Study

MDA TRAINING

Background

Management Development Associates (MDA) was set up in 1988 by Professor Walter Reid of London Business School, initially as a business training consultancy for financial analysts. Since then, it has developed and broadened into a general commerce training consultancy and currently employs some 30 staff. Rather than focusing on the softer skills of management, MDA directs its efforts at training delegates in the harder skills (business finance, e-commerce, business management, marketing and business strategy), which are seen by MDA's clients to add more value.

MDA considers its key strength to be in the design of courseware for clients. Its aim is to 'help businesses to achieve their objectives by enhancing managers' business knowledge and skills'.

It also seeks to deliver innovation in programme design and imaginative, intelligent training solutions to business problems.

Examining the case for e-learning

MDA's view is that it will use e-commerce and e-learning when it is a cost-effective and an appropriate vehicle for training. MDA considers that it would make more sense to use e-learning in testing knowledge and skills rather than for training staff in the conventional sense.

MDA is considering using computer-based training (CBT) to test delegates prior to their attendance on a training course. By determining the level of knowledge of each delegate prior to the course, it would therefore be possible to tailor the course to the correct level, or to provide supplementary material to those delegates who may be in need of additional advance tuition. The need for a 'lecture-style' training course where information is conveyed to the delegates could then be eliminated and the training course could focus its energies on providing scenarios and interaction between the delegates.

Despite the increasing availability of online learning, MDA considers it more as an 'additional tool in the training kitbag'. MDA argues that you cannot replicate interaction between delegates within the classroom. The synergy of an 'offline event' cannot be replicated. The course structure being used by MDA relies on facilitation by participants, and by removing this, the challenge of the classroom is also removed.

Computer-based training has not been hugely successful in this market. Many of MDA's clients who had used CBT as a learning tool are reverting to the classroom format. This may be due to the participant opinion of CBT as being 'something they have to get through' and boring to undertake. Some organisations have, in the past, prescribed a certain amount of CBT to their staff. In reality, many may find it tiresome to complete and therefore do not necessarily learn the material and do not know where to apply this knowledge.

Generally, MDA sees e-learning packages as useful for disseminating information (especially technical information) that can be digested at the participant's leisure. It should, however, be sup-plemented by a classroom-style event to encourage interaction between the participants.

Reviewing e-learning packages

When evaluating e-learning packages, MDA has found that it is important to consider the following:

- *Cost* – in implementing e-learning packages, there is consider-able expense up front in designing and programming a suit-able package for clients. However, in the long run, such packages are cheaper than classroom-based activities, as updates are relatively easy once the initial system has been set up.
- *Value added* – although cheaper, CBT is viewed as being of lower value added to the organisation. As was mentioned previously, some clients have abandoned the use of CBT because participants found it laborious. MDA would argue that classroom activity is of higher quality. However, MDA would support the use of e-learning as a supplement to exist-ing classroom-based training because it would ultimately shorten the training time and, as a result, participants would be out of work for a shorter period of time.
- *Availability of technical expertise* – since technical expertise is of paramount importance in considering CBT's use, MDA is presently considering a number of options:
  - *in-house resources* – this is an expensive option, since train-ing an existing member of staff results in time away from running training programmes to acquire the complex technical skills and knowledge necessary to write and develop appropriate packages
  - recruitment of technical staff who already possess the knowledge and expertise to write and develop computer packages
  - the creation of a joint venture with an online business by which MDA would provide the content and the partner organisation would provide the design and technical back-up.

Summary

MDA considers e-learning not to be an entirely new concept and disputes whether it would always be the best way to train people. Ideally, therefore, MDA prefers second-mover advantage and does not seek to be at the forefront of this technological advancement. By learning from others' mistakes and difficulties, a more user-friendly product can be established. There is a great deal of cynicism surrounding a 'one-stop shop' for training. MDA continues to support the use of classroom events, as these allow participant interaction and consolidation of learning.

Despite these reservations, MDA believes that it would be useful to offer some form of online learning material and to promote an ongoing learning intervention. However, it is important to consider the cost and value of this form of intervention. Buyers of this type of product are invariably sophisticated and know what they want and who the players in this market are. The material contained in packages is 'only as good as the people put-ting in the information'. This leads to a question of quality of the courseware. It is easier to use CBT for disseminating knowledge, but it is not appropriate for developing skills. In short, MDA does not consider e-learning to offer a one-stop shop for training.

My thanks to Chris Stuart of MDA for his assistance in the prep-aration of this case study.

Case Study

DOVE NEST GROUP

Background

Dove Nest is a small management development consultancy group based in the Lake District of England. Founded 20 years ago, it describes itself as one of the country's leaders in manage-ment, organisational and team development. Dove Nest consists of a number of closely linked companies which together provide the full range of management development services.

Dove Nest has expertise in a number of subject areas (including leadership, team development, strategic business development and coaching) and aims to provide a highly effective learning environment away from the workplace where management problems can be simulated.

Recently, Dove Nest Group has been piloting new initiatives for clients that will enhance their performance as individuals and within teams. Two are of particular interest: the provision of an online 360-degree feedback questionnaire and a website dedicated to team development (www.teamkinetics.com).

Online 360-degree feedback
In November 1999, Dove Nest proposed to design and market a 360-degree feedback questionnaire as an intervention for one of its clients that would feed into its performance management process. The initial idea was to create a questionnaire that would be completed online by staff members and subsequently returned using the Internet. Its introduction was intended to reduce the need for paper, speed up returns and avoid unnecessary clogging of postal and fax facilities. The initial investment in this venture was £3,000 (aside from the internal cost to Dove Nest for resources).

In order to develop this solution, Dove Nest employed an IT firm as a subcontractor. The design involved input from managers within the client company and was created from 360-degree feedback questionnaires based on the client's competency framework. To operate this system, users would be able to access the questionnaires through customised Internet portals using hidden files and password protection.

The system was tested using individual machines and results showed that the system was running well. The finished product was introduced to the clients in April 2000 and, despite the tests, ran into the following problems with the client:

- the client's IT network blocked any responses from being sent out; the client could therefore access the system but could not send its returns via the Internet – the clients ended up having to print out their forms and return them by post
- difficulties arose keeping track of the respondents
- people clicked on the wrong boxes, leading to incorrect responses
- staff who had four superiors ended up with a mountain of questionnaires to complete
- the forms were designed as a standard, but the output had to be generated in a form that could feed straight into a spread-sheet to generate scores.

In retrospect, Dove Nest believes that had it approached the IT problem differently, it would have been possible to pre-empt the problems with the client IT networks. Other issues could then have been overcome more quickly. The group is working on these problems for the future, and the system is eagerly awaited by the client.

The website
In March 2000, Dove Nest launched a website dedicated to team development. This site has been named www.teamkinetics.com. The advent of more powerful technology and the increase in 'virtual' teamworking (where members of the team no longer have to be in the same location but can communicate via e-mail, telephone and video-conferencing) have led to a unique set of team learning and development issues. The site aims to provide 'team solutions for e-business and dynamic businesses' whereby the group will work with clients to design team architecture and develop teams capable of high performance in a dynamic environment. Indeed, the site proposes to be an 'interactive site to enable companies to find solutions from team architecture to teamworking'.

The site was introduced to demonstrate that Dove Nest Group could design and support team activity in companies (particularly the dot.com companies). The group has initially invested approximately two weeks of work in its own time and resources and a further £500 of external costs in this venture.

At present the site is in its early stages. Indeed, the interactivity of the site has not yet been established and information is stored for purely marketing and relationship-building purposes. In creating this site, Dove Nest has also encountered problems linking the name of the site (and its contents) to Internet search engines to make it possible for Internet users and potential clients to find the site by browsing the Internet. As a result, gaining client exposure is more difficult. However, once the site is fully established, marketing the proposal will be far easier and faster, as it is relatively easy to improve and update the site once it is in existence.

The ideal for Dove Nest is to be able to provide online provision of consultancy for team development 24 hours a day. It proposes to do this by forming partnerships with other worldwide providers of a similar service. The result would be 'globalisation' of the site and a name that clients would recognise across the world. The site would not simply provide a database of information on team development but there would be a 'virtual' consultant available online to answer queries, derive solutions and assist/facilitate in team development.

This idea may be more attainable than initial impressions suggest. Time differences in countries around the world would make it possible for a consultant to be available 24 hours a day. The most difficult aspect of creating will be finding organisations to form a global partnership and in marketing the site to the global audience.

The future of e-learning at Dove Nest
The two examples represent early responses to the opportunity of e-learning. Several problems have been encountered in launching them and Dove Nest is working on overcoming them. Dove Nest has highlighted the need for using a reputable technology firm in creating online provision of learning and development interventions. Knowledge and expertise in this area of technology is important to ensure that possible problems can be pre-empted. It is continuing to develop its online initiatives, buying in expertise where necessary (there is no time for self-discovery with this type of ever-advancing technology).

The dramatic increase in online business and e-business solutions has resulted in a rapid increase in virtual teamworking and work situations that are unfamiliar to employees. Dove Nest is keen to assist companies in their development by deriving appropriate learning interventions for this dynamic marketplace. However, in practical terms, as David Moore, managing director of Dove Nest Group, puts it: 'We may need to wait for technology to catch up.'

My thanks to Dave Moore for his assistance in the preparation of this case study.

Chapter 8

Trainers and the new economy

When you come to a fork in the road, take it

The previous chapter considered the effect that the new economic environment will have on the training industry. In this chapter some wider social issues will be discussed. At their heart is a beguilingly simple question: 'Are the new opportunities for improved training a good thing for society?'

‹The market for training will become more efficient›

A straightforward uncritical positive response should be resisted. There are a number of implications to be considered. It is unquestionably true that, in common with everything that the Internet affects, the market for training will become more efficient. It is equally true that the balance of power will shift to the consumer – the learner who is the user of training. However, there are some important social issues to be considered on the distribution of access to training opportunities. This raises the question of whether human resource professionals should seek to take an active position on the social issues or should remain passive players merely responding to the changing forces that influence the training market.

These questions will be the subject of this chapter. The underlying proposition is

Proposition 20

Social inclusion is emerging as a key political issue. Trainers have the power to influence the debate positively.

It is hard to gainsay the argument that the issue of social inclusion is a legitimate concern for government. What is less certain is what it may or may not have to do with trainers – save in their capacity as individual electors.

The premise underlying this chapter is that it should be of concern. Trainers should, as citizens, be concerned about social inclusion, and with the arrival of the connected economy, the trainer has a unique opportunity to make a positive contribution.

Inclusion, access and distribution

In its report on the future of training technology,[1] the American Society for Training and Development included the following observation from the American novelist William Gibson: 'The future's already arrived – it's just not evenly distributed yet.'[2]

Certainly the better examples of the application of e-learning described in the case studies in this book could be said to offer a glimpse of the future for some individuals in some organisations. However, there are many issues to be considered before concluding that e-learning for all is a universal panacea.

E-learning has the potential to bring enormous benefits to a great number of individuals. This is true of all applications of the Internet. However, as with any significant economic change, there is a change in the balance of power. Some organisations and some individuals gain at the expense of others.

‛Divisions based on technology could prove more intractable than the ideological divisions of the Cold War›

There is a whole range of potentially disadvantaged groups whose position should be recognised. Far and away the most important issue is international disparities surrounding access to technology. Jeffrey Sachs, Harvard Professor of International Trade, writing in *The Economist*[3] presents a powerful case for this proposition. He argues that divisions based on technology could prove more intractable than the ideological divisions of the Cold War:

> A small part of the globe, accounting for some 15% of the Earth's population, provides nearly all of the world's technology innovations. A second, involving perhaps half of the world's population, is able to adopt these technologies in production and consumption. The remaining part, covering around a third of the world's population, is technology-disconnected, neither innovating at home nor adopting foreign technologies.

Professor Sachs argues that unless action is taken, the divisions will become greater: regions with the advanced technologies are best placed to innovate further and have access to larger markets. He suggests that three things need to happen:

> First, the new technology-driven character of the global economy must be thought through: geography, public health and ecology must be brought into the analysis of technological change and economic growth. Second, governments need to change their approach to aid, spending more and more wisely. Third, participation in informational assistance needs to be broadened and recast. Multinational firms and First-World universities and scientific establishments need to be engaged, and the official agencies charged with global development (the IMF, the World Bank, and the various UN agencies) must be reformed. (p113)

This is a demanding agenda, but the problem is critical. Action is needed if the 2 billion people who live in these technologically disconnected regions are to benefit from globalisation.

The domestic problems in the UK surrounding inclusion, access and distribution pale by comparison. However, if web-based training does develop as expected, it is possible to identify three potential categories of the 'e-learning-disconnected':

- people who, by virtue of the nature of their employment (or non-employment), will not get access to training opportunities and self-development through e-learning
- people who are computer-phobic
- organisations that are not, and will not be, at the leading edge because they do not have the ability to invest in the technology.

All three of these categories could properly be seen as the concern of the government. However, a brief comment should be offered on the third point. Although there is some truth in the suggestion that there may be e-learning-disconnected organisations, this should not be a focus of significant concern. This view is offered for the following reasons, which reflect many of the arguments developed throughout this book. First, there will be few organisations in the UK who will manage without an effective technology platform of some kind. Second, the demand for e-learning will lead to the emergence of vendors or suppliers who will offer suitable products or solutions for smaller organisations. Third, as the stream of case studies throughout this book has demonstrated, the case for adopting the all-powerful e-learning system is still to be proven. For some organisations it may be appropriate to invest in such a system; for others the case will be far from self-evident. The market will develop and change. The more appropriate focus for concern should be the disadvantaged individual.

Access and inclusion: the Ufi

A full summary and critique of government training policy falls outside the scope of this book, which is concerned with articulating the forward agenda. However, a brief outline of one important initiative, the University for Industry (Ufi), forms the next section of this chapter.

The 1997 general election resulted in the defeat of the Conservative Government and its replacement by a new Labour administration. Prime Minister Tony Blair's famous sound bite on priorities, 'education, education, education', may well have been intended to embrace corporate training. Plans had been signalled by the publication, in March 1996, of a policy document entitled *Labour's Plans for a Skills Revolution*.

The 1996 publication contained three distinct sets of proposals: the introduction of 'Learn as you Earn' accounts; a new stimulus for the Investors in People programme (and a way of making it accessible for smaller organisations); and the establishment of a University for Industry.

On achieving office, the new Labour Government signalled a commitment to the concept of lifelong learning. In a green paper pub-

lished in 1998, the government advocated support for a culture of
lifelong learning and the creation of a framework of opportunities for
people to learn.[4] The establishment of what was seen then as a 'virtual' or electronic University for Industry (Ufi) was part of this framework. The initial pathfinder prospectus, also issued in 1998,
suggested that the university should act as a broker (providing refer-
ral services), as a change agent (publishing the value of lifelong learning for adults) and as a directing force (investigating skills shortages
and co-ordinating actions to deal with them). It would rely solely on
open and distance learning: it would concentrate on priority areas
where there are large-scale demands and reflect national strategic
needs. These needs concerned the basic skills of literacy and numeracy; information and communication technologies in the workplace;
small and medium-sized businesses; and four specified sectors of the
economy. Targets were bold; it was intended that by 2002 Ufi services would be used by 2.5 million individuals and employers.

The Ufi was established in April 1997 as a limited company independent of the government, but with the government as a major stake-
holder providing funding allocation during the development phases.
The term 'learndirect' was adopted as the Ufi consumer-facing brand,
and the nationwide network of online learning services are being marketed using that brand name. The ambitions and challenges facing
learndirect are of considerable interest in the context of this book – and
of particular relevance to this chapter. **learndirect**, therefore, is the
subject of the final case study set out at the end of this chapter. It can
be seen that the pledge to learners reproduced in the case study should
be regarded as a firm declaration of learner-centred interventions.

A professional response: open source

At the start of this chapter it was suggested that with the arrival of
the connected economy, the training profession has a unique opportunity to make a positive contribution to issues on inclusion. In fact,
the challenge facing the training profession is much broader: encouraging greater inclusion is one of a series of issues facing the profession. Another is the case for co-operation.

Arguments surrounding professional co-operation are complex. They
concern the extent to which a group should seek to act as a group to

make its product or skills more widely available as a matter of principle. An apt illustration may prove more helpful than a philosophical discussion at this stage. The illustration is drawn from information technology, particularly the writing of Tim Berners-Lee and the open-source movement.

As noted in Chapter 1, Tim Berners-Lee worked at CERN, the European Organisation for Nuclear Research (the subject of the case study included in Chapter 4, pages 87–91). In the early 1990s he designed the basic software infrastructure for communication that led to the Internet: he has been justifiably described as the Internet's inventor. In 1999 he wrote, with a co-author, a book entitled *Weaving the Web*. His book is of interest for two reasons: first, because of the historical account of the development of the Internet; second, because much of the book deals with his belief that openness of standards and of access is the appropriate way forward for the Web.

Tim Berners-Lee's idealism shines through his book:

> My original vision for a universal Web was an armchair aid to help people do things in the web of real life. It would be a mirror, reflecting reports or conversations or art and mapping social interactions. But more and more, the mirror model is wrong, because interaction is taking place primarily on the Web. People are using the Web to build things they have not built or written or drawn or communicated anywhere else. As the Web becomes a primary space for much activity, we have to be careful that it allows for a just and fair society. The Web must allow equal access to those in different economic and political situations; those who have physical or cognitive disabilities, those of different cultures; and those who use different languages with different characters that read in different directions across a page.[5] (p178)

One practical result of this idealism is that all web code (the lines of programming) has been open-source software. Anyone can access, use, edit and rebuild the code. 'Open source' has developed into a movement with adherents from the software movement. Its philosophy is of interest at this stage of the book.

Open source is basically software developed by unco-ordinated but collaborating programmers, using freely distributed source and the communications of the Internet. The open-source movement consists of individuals who believe that open-source development creates better software than can be developed in a corporate or proprietary environment.

The very nature of the open-source movement means that it is hard to identify a simple cohesive strand. On the other hand, not unexpectedly, there is a wealth of information, discussion and analysis available on the Web.[6]

Chris DiBona *et al*, writing an introduction to the open-source movement,[7] begin with a consideration of the circumstances that led to the discovery of the structure of DNA. There was a strong competitive element and some ethical issues over secrecy. James Watson, who together with Francis Crick made the crucial breakthrough, felt uncomfortable with the need for secrecy: he felt that professional competition led to a delay in disclosing information, and the progress of science was affected. DiBona *et al* summarise:

> Science, after all, is ultimately an Open-Source enterprise. The scientific method rests on the process of discovery, and a process of justification. For scientific results to be justified, they must be replicable. Replication is not possible unless the source is shared: the hypothesis, the test conditions, and the results. The process of discovery can follow many paths, and at times scientific discoveries do occur in isolation. But ultimately the process of discovery must be served by sharing information: enabling other scientists to go forward where one cannot; pollinating the ideas of others so that something new may grow that otherwise would not have been born.

The philosophical approach here can easily be extended to software. To quote from the opensource.org webpage:[6]

> The basic idea behind open source is very simple. When programmers on the Internet can read, redistribute and modify the source for a piece of software, it evolves. People improve it, people adapt it, people fix bugs. And this can happen at a speed that, if one is used to the slow pace of conventional software development, seems astonishing.

> We in the open-source community have learned that this rapid evolutionary process produces better software than the traditional closed model, in which only a very few programmers can see source and everybody else must blindly use an opaque block of bits.

‘Open-source development creates better software than can be developed in a corporate or proprietary environment’

Shared development of software, then, is more effective and it produces a better end result. Open-source development, runs the argument, creates better software than can be developed in a corporate or proprietary environment. It is more robust and can be better supported and more innovative. This has led to a number of developments to promote initiatives designed to put such beliefs into practice.

The open-source movement has many strands. An underlying issue to be considered is the commercial imperative that must drive many producers of software. If sharing of information is a good thing socially, how could commercial organisations be encouraged to share? In the early stages of the debate, a researcher at MIT, Richard Stallman, advocated an approach based on ‘free software’. This was software where the developers permit users the freedom to:

- run the program for any purpose
- study how the program works, and adapt it
- redistribute copies
- improve the program, and release improvements so that the whole community benefits.

Access to the source code is necessarily a precondition for this (see www.gnu.org).

In 1997 a group of developers met to consider the implications and raise the profile of free software. One key decision was an agreement to use the term ‘open-source software’ rather than ‘free software’. This term assists by emphasising the critical underlying distinction: such software must be non-proprietary (open to distribution and development), not necessarily non-commercial – developers and distributors may charge for their service. Organisations and individuals may, through offering a value-added service, generate income through software that is licensed open source.

The most prominent subsequent development has been the emergence of Linux – an operating system developed initially by Linus Torvalds, a student at the University of Helsinki. This has emerged as a significant competitor to Microsoft operating systems. It was developed by a loosely knit group of programmers, is downloaded from the Internet at no charge, and can be distributed and modified. It is licensed under an open-source public licence, and companies and developers may charge as long as the open-source principles are observed.[8]

The professional agenda for trainers

The open-source movement is a professional response to the issues raised by inclusion, access and distribution at a time of disruptive technology. Readers may wish to reflect whether there are analogies between open-source software and training models. Should, for example, the profession seek to develop a set of tools designed to assist individuals to acquire basic skills and make them freely available?

The difficulty here is that the human resource profession generally and trainers in particular have been reluctant to take a stance – and such stances have tended not to go beyond 'learning is a good thing'. This is doubtless one of the attractions of the rather woolly concept of the learning organisation that was outlined in Chapter 3 (pages 58–62). In 1998, a group of leading thinkers on learning in organisations produced and promulgated a declaration on learning.[9] There was much to welcome in the declaration: among the signatories were a number of people whose work has been cited in the course of this volume. However, the intervention does not seem to have provided a sustained debate in the profession or led to any new activity.

This section will conclude with two suggestions for actions that professionals could take now. The first is more general and is addressed to the trainers as individuals; the second requires concerted or group action. Where they are potentially controversial is that they are not market-neutral. The suggestions, particularly the second, would lead to activity that could affect the shape of the emerging market for e-learning.

The first suggestion is set out in the final proposition.

Proposition 21

More honesty and less hype is required if the training profession is to grasp the new opportunity to maximum effect.

‹ The long-term credibility of the profession may depend on an honest appraisal of successes and failures ›

This proposition suggests that propaganda should not drive the debate. There is plenty for trainers to achieve and a great deal of satisfaction to be gained without overstating the potential advantages to be derived from e-learning. More importantly, the long-term credibility of the profession, at this stage of transition, may depend on an honest appraisal of successes and failures.

At present much of the emphasis on e-learning is on marketing. Conference organisers are busily promoting events that combine contributions from trainer managers and industry experts. It is in the corporate training manager's personal and professional interest to give a positive gloss to events. It is obviously more palatable to present a case study as a success. High profile does not, however, necessarily mean successful embedding of product or process. To introduce a lighter note, no one has as yet, as far as this author is aware, offered the sort of conference case study parodied in Focus Point 33.

It is evidently in the interests of suppliers or vendors of technology-based learning products to give the best impression of the acceptance of their products. This combined marketing effect from training managers and vendors may detract attention from the need for a hard-edged evaluation of results and shaping of information if e-learning is to be embedded effectively.

If this all seems unduly cynical, consider the following. First, in the author's experience, the age of computer-based training (CBT) and CD-ROMs led to purchases of material that did not find sufficient

Focus Point 33: The conference paper we will never see

Gareth Holmes is training manager of Lakin Scott Golding, a firm of 3,000 people with two manufacturing sites and one head-quarters site in south-east England.

In 1999, due to cost pressures, Lakin Scott Golding switched from predominantly classroom training to electronically based training delivered through CBT and later the company intranet. The result was chaos and, in this session, Gareth Holmes will describe how:

- incompatibility of IT systems and the chosen products led to huge overruns and how the launch and promotion was delayed three times
- a learning cafe was set up and how it rapidly degenerated into a badly maintained spare meeting room
- many of the soft-skill modules available on the system were used once by participants and found to be both trivial in content and difficult to access
- a series of cottage industries developed in parts of the business where concerned managers sent their staff on un-authorised external courses, with a resulting lack of budgetary control.

Gareth Holmes, an experienced speaker at conferences, is soon to establish a consultancy specialising in change management.

[NOTE: Gareth Holmes and Lakin Scott Golding are purely ficti-tious, and any resemblance to individuals or organisations is purely coincidental.]

acceptance with many users and is now littering cupboards the length and breadth of the land. Second, it proved extremely difficult to find case studies for this book. On a number of occasions training vendors were asked if they could assist by facilitating introductions to training managers who were using their systems. The initial response was invariably helpful and positive; the final result was often a message that, at this stage, it was too early to share any infor-mation. This makes my gratitude to those who did participate by providing case studies, and the honesty of their responses, even more profound.

A third point leads to a specific suggestion. In the course of the research for this book, hard information on time and space to learn proved most elusive. Such information that was obtained on the new approaches to learning is set out in Chapter 5. There is evidently a paucity of relevant research to assist the training manager in the age of e-learning. The key questions on how, when and where individuals prefer to learn were set out in Focus Point 21 (page 126). In this author's view there is an evident need for a repository where trainers can share the answers and ideas.

The second specific suggestion, therefore, is that trainers should establish, as a matter of urgency, a community site to share information issues on the introduction of e-learning. The idea of a community was defined in Chapter 2 where learning systems were considered (see Figure 3 and accompanying discussion on pages 44–47). More generally, community sites are a growing feature of Internet activity. They can provide users with sources of news, current information and ideas. Most of these sites are commercially run: they offer an opportunity to buy relevant products for the community (machine tools for the engineering community: office equipment for small businesses, for example); many contain job advertisements.

At HRD 2000 – the annual training and development conference and exhibition organised by the CIPD for that year – two competing training 'exchange' sites were on display. Both offered training managers free access to a market in training courses from a number of suppliers. What is proposed here is different: this is the establishment of a community site for training managers to assist them in the introduction of e-learning. The business proposition should be built around this intention but the site must be vendor-neutral. The obvious organisation to establish the site is the Chartered Institute of Personnel and Development.

Training, education and the new opportunity

To some readers this discussion on inclusion will seem an irrelevance; to others it is of considerable importance. To those in the second group, two brief interpolations may appeal.

The first is simply the memorial on the tombstone of an eighteenth-century Norfolk blacksmith who was buried some three miles from where this book was written:

> Johnson Jex/Born in obscurity he passed his days at Letheringsett/A village blacksmith/By the force of an original and inventive genius/Combined with indomitable perseverance/He mastered some of the greatest difficulties of science/Advancing from the forge to the crucible/And from the horse-shoe to the chronometer/Acquiring by mental labour/And philosophic research/A vast and varied amount of mechanical skill/And general knowledge/He was a man of scrupulous integrity/But regardless of wealth/And insensitive to the voice of fame/He lived and died a scientific anchorite/Aged 73

The second interpolation concerns a more recent event. While on my way to a meeting with a training manager to research one of the case studies, I left a central London tube station. A man whom I recognised but could not place rushed up to me with a grin and exchanged greetings. Realisation dawned: it was the former *Big Issue* salesman at my local station. He had held the pitch successfully for 12 months, but had then moved on to work as the area manager. I took the opportunity to ask him how he had become homeless when he was so reliable: he explained his circumstances, but this was clearly now well in the past. He said that he was very pleased to see his old customers and hoped all was well with me but had to dash. The polite and unspoken yet firm implication was that I might have time on my hands at the moment, whereas he had things to do.

How are these interpolations relevant to the themes of this book? The fact is simply that, for many people, training and education are rather special goods and interventions. The acquisition of job-related skills gives people pride in their work: they can acquire new confidence and self-respect. Johnson Jex achieved his immense accomplishments without e-learning – but what would he have made of the Internet? In the case of the former *Big Issue* salesman, an intervention had made a great deal of difference to his life – and this intervention included powerful training elements. If e-learning allows us to undertake training interventions more effectively, it is an innovation that must be of considerable benefit to all.

In short there is an ethical dimension to all of this. This book began with a dedication to all those who hold schoolteacher values. These values are about creating and sharing, rather than exploiting new opportunities solely for personal advantage. May e-learning develop in this tradition.

References

1   ABERNATHY D., ALLERTON H., BARRON T. *and* SALOPEK J. 'Trendz'. *Training and Development*, November 1999.

2   I am grateful to Pat Galagan, editor-in-chief of *Training and Development*, for drawing my attention to this quotation.

3   SACHS J. 'Sachs on globalisation: a new map of the world'. *The Economist*. 24 June 2000. pp113–15.

4   'The learning age: a renaissance for a new Britain'. Cmd 3970, Government Green Paper. London, The Stationery Office, 1998.

5   BERNERS-LEE T. *with* FISCHETTI M. *Weaving the Web*. London, Orion Business Books, 1999.

6   On the open-source movement see: http://release1.edventure. com/index.cfm; www.gnu.org/philosophy; and www.opensource. org/.

7   DiBONA C., OCKMAN S. *and* STONE M. 'Introduction'. In DiBona C. and Ockman S. *Open Sources: Voices from the open source revolution*. Farnham, O'Reilly & Associates, 1999. See also www.oreilly.com/catalog/opensources/book/intro.html.

8   See www.linux.com.

9   HONEY P. 'The debate starts here (a declaration on learning)'. *People Management*. 1 October 1998. pp28–9.

Case Study

LEARNDIRECT

Objectives

In articulating its vision, Ufi made a firm commitment to 'put the learner at the heart of our operation and to seek to put the learner first'. The following learning principles were presented in the vision document, published in May 2000:

We promise:

> To offer the time, place, pace and style of learning that responds to their needs.
>
> To give clear information that helps them make the best personal choices about the learning programmes and maintain control of them.
>
> To enable them to monitor their progress and record their achievements as they go, not just at the end of a complete programme.
>
> The opportunity, on completion of a set of **learndirect** learning materials, to present evidence of their achievements for credit towards the widest range of nationally recognised qualifications.
>
> Easy access to the specialist support they need.
>
> To put them in touch with other people studying the same topics.
>
> To give them the chance to relate their learning to their own longer-term ambitions.

Such promises, summarised as Ufi's pledge to learners, are ambitious. They go beyond making materials available anytime, anywhere. They commit the organisation to providing the individual learner with appropriate resources and support.

The approach

Ufi faced some important decisions on the delivery of its service. On content, it has sought to give existing suppliers of learning materials every opportunity to provide against specifications determined by its commissioning managers. As a publicly funded body, clear tender specifications and purchasing procedures are applied. Ufi is not entering the business of the design and development of materials. Not surprisingly in what is the rapidly developing field of e-learning, Ufi is, however, commissioning new learning materials to fill gaps in the market and to enable it to make available materials in the sectors that are its prime targets. This has proved necessary so far for basic skills (numeracy, literacy and English as a second language), environmental services and technology, retail and distribution, and also for the small and middle-sized enterprise (SME) sector. In addition, some existing distance-learning products have required enhancements to ensure they meet Ufi's standards.

A consortium led by the software house Logica is developing a system to support a nationwide network of learning hubs and centres (see below). Integrated software is being commissioned to meet the requirements of a range of users – from individual learners to staff and content providers.

A particularly important decision concerns the initial creation of up to 100 local hubs – these will co-ordinate the activity of learndirect learning centres. It is planned that the number will rise to up to 1,000. A learning hub is a local consortium made up of learning providers and employers, and will have strong links with the local community. Some sort of educational institute must be involved, so that the hub can access the government funding for learners available to higher or further education colleges.

Learner access and support

Given its ambitions, which must be seen in the wider social context of the government's intentions on access to learning delivery, learner support poses a major challenge.

Part of the response lies in the decision to make learning available as discrete modules. In the early stages, over 250 courses were available – over 80 per cent of them online. These courses were designed to provide 'bite-sized chunks' of learning of perhaps 20 minutes' duration.

The price charged to learners will be determined by the learning hubs, which will take into account operating costs, local demand and the public funding available for any particular course. In the earliest stages, Ufi learning materials were made available to the hubs without charge, and subsequently a pricing tariff was applied. Ufi expects the smaller, bite-sized chunks of learning to be available to users at as little as £8. Longer courses could typically cost between £100 and £200 depending on how many hours' learning is involved. Many courses will be eligible for funding from further education bodies; basic skills courses and some information and communication technology (ICT) courses will be free.

Most importantly the aim is to fit learning opportunities into an individual's lifestyle: to make learning accessible on an either individual or community basis according to preferences.

Currently, individuals must first register at a learndirect centre (they are also able to register online), but can proceed from there in a number of ways. At one extreme they can work alone and have no access to the learning centre – all courses are designed to be used as stand-alone, self-managed modules. If, on the other hand, they choose to visit a learndirect centre, they will receive support in terms of induction and assistance to get them started and to give them confidence. In larger centres designated learner facilitators will be available to offer more specific advice in using the general suite of courses.

Beyond this, Ufi has plans to introduce learner-to-learner dialogue in the form of chat rooms. It has also recruited moderators who will assist by online interventions designed to promote effective learning. A copy of the advertisement/job specification for the role of learning moderator was reproduced in Focus Point 26 on pages 153–4.

All learners will have logs, which they may use to record their learning and hopefully will prove to be of value on their career development. A completed log could be included in job applications or submitted at job interviews.

Given the range of learners and preferences, it is reasonable to ask whether learndirect can possibly meet all their needs. A very open model has been developed and Ufi is comfortable with the possibility that the organisation could develop in a number of different ways. Institutions and organisations associated with a learning hub could develop far closer associations and combine arrangements for delivery and support, for example. The learndirect model is still in its early stages: a range of materials geared to a potential range of learners has been developed. Efforts will be made to access learner needs and to support them accordingly. A substantial sum has been set aside to research learner preference: no prior assumptions on learner styles have been made.

It is hard, at this early stage, to do anything other than to wish learndirect well and watch its activities with considerable interest. Undoubtedly, important lessons will be learned – both by the organisation and by individual learners.

My thanks to Dr Mary Benwell, Director of Learning, and to Ufi for their assistance in the preparation of this case study.

References

Ufi. *Vision of the Way Ahead.* Sheffield, University for Industry, 2000. See www.ufiltd.co.uk/corporateplan/index.htm.

Index

abstract conceptualisation 117
acceptability of e-learning 124–5
access to e-learning 180–83
    disadvantaged categories 181–2
    international disparities 180–81
    University for Industry 182–3
activists (learning style) 119
agenda for e-learning, determination
    of 82–4
American Society for Training and
    Development (ASTD) 38–41,
    56–7, 145–6, 148
Argyris, Chris 58
Asch, David 152
asynchronous learning 114, 115, 151

bandwidth 11, 90
barriers to learning 121
Bassi, Laurie J. 38
BBC Online (case study) 14, 20–23
Berge, Zane 114
Berners-Lee, Tim 2, 184
blurring 12–14, 37, 64–5
borderless education 37
British Airways (case study) 122,
    134–7
broadband Internet connections 11
budgeting 78–9, 163–4

Cap Gemini Ernst & Young (case
    study) 48–52
    see also Ernst & Young
career networks 9

case studies
    BBC Online 20–23
    British Airways 134–7
    Cap Gemini Ernst & Young
        48–52
    CERN 87–91
    Clifford Chance 97–100
    Dove Nest Group 174–8
    Ernst & Young 72–4
    Hanover Housing Association
        91–6
    IBM 105–7
    learndirect 192–6
    Management Development
        Associates (MDA) 171–4
    Motorola 131–4
    The Post Office 100–104
CD-ROMs 36, 121
    extent of usage 38, 39
    limitations of 85
CERN (case study) 2, 87–91
Chartered Institute of Personnel and
    Development 190
    see also (prior to July 2000)
        Institute of Personnel and
        Development
Christensen, Clayton 4, 6, 36
classroom learning 85–6, 110–13,
    125, 172
    see also virtual classrooms
clickstream data 165, 166
Clifford Chance (case study)
    97–100

CMC *see* computer-mediated
    conferencing
coaching
    definition of 155
    Motorola case study 134
commodity markets 7
'common knowledge' 66–7
community
    learning system architecture 45, 46
    websites 190
    see also group support
competition, effects of Internet on
    6–8, 10
competitive advantage, derived from
    human resources 25–30, 61,
    62, 64
computer-mediated conferencing
    151–2
'cone of experience' 146
conjoint analysis 124
connected economy 6–19
    blur concept 12–14
    definition of term 4
    e-commerce 3, 10–12, 17
    implications for trainers 4, 6,
        9–10, 12, 18–19
    new business models 15–18,
        159–60
connectivity
    and blur concept 12–13, 14–15
    definition of term 4
    see also connected economy
consumer e-commerce 10–12
content of learning systems 46
'content agnostic' systems 46
copyright *see* intellectual property
corporate universities 33–5, 37
    Cap Gemini Ernst & Young
        case study 48–52
    Motorola case study 131–4
costing e-learning 78–9, 163
counselling 155
Cross, J. 41
customisation of learning systems 46

Dale, Edgar 146
Daniel, Sir John 111
Davis, Stan 12–13, 61, 76
design and development roles in
    e-learning 146, 148–9
DiBona, C. 185
digital collaboration 149–50

digital surrounds 43
directive approaches to training 55
'disintermediation' 12
'disruptive technology' 4, 6
Dixon, Nancy 66
double-loop organisational learning
    58–9
Dove Nest Group (case study) 174–8
Driscoll, Marcy 113, 120

e-commerce
    Economist survey 10–12
    projected growth of 3
    as stage in business
        transformation 17
    see also connected economy
e-companies 17
e-learning
    acceptability to learners 124–5
    definition of term 3, 5
    determining agenda for 82–4
    extent of implementation in
        UK 32–3
    extent of implementation in
        USA 38–40
    future trends 39, 41, 46–7
    implementation principles 76,
        80, 81
    learners as focus of 42–3, 45
    need for more information and
        evaluation 188–90
    transformation matrix for 79–81
    work of Elliott Masie 42–4
e-learning systems *see* learning
    systems
e-moderating 144, 150–52, 153–4
e-training *see* e-learning
e-transformation 14–18
Economist (The) 10–12
Ellison, Larry 1
employability 30, 70
employees, as source of competitive
    advantage 25–30, 61, 62, 64
Employment National Training
    Organisation 140
Ernst & Young 15, 30, 78, 79, 120,
    154, 163, 165
    case study 72–4
    learning portal questionnaire
        127, 128–30
    see also Cap Gemini Ernst &
    Young

European Organization for Nuclear
    Research *see* CERN
evaluation of training 165
experiential learning 86
extranets 4

facilitation of online groups *see*
    e-moderating
facilitation role of training
    professionals 139, 141–2
feedback
    in performance management
        systems 72–4, 175–6
    from training course participants
        165–70
'fit' of learning systems 143, 144
Forrester Research 8–9, 10
frameworks *see* single frames;
    transformation frameworks;
    transmission frameworks
free software 186
*Fund management: new skills for
    a new age* 8
Future of corporate learning (The) 34

government policy 182–3
group support
    e-moderating 144, 150–52,
        153–4
    self-managed learning groups
        154, 156
groupware 74

Hanover Housing Association (case
    study) 91–6
hard technology 45, 111, 142
Harvard Business School 161
Henley Management College 49
High Performance Management
    On-Line 161
'high touch' 11, 40, 42, 144–5,
    162
higher education, changes in 37
Honey, Peter 117–18
human capital 60, 61

I-cubed *see* Intranet Immediate
    Instruction
IBM
    case study 86, 105–7
    research on learner acceptability
        124–5

implementation of e-learning
    general principles 76, 80, 81
    roles in 146, 147
inclusion, issues on 179–83
information issues 190
infrastructure of learning systems 46
Institute of Personnel and
    Development
    knowledge management research
        62–3
    training surveys 31–2
    see also (from July 2000) Chartered
        Institute of Personnel and
        Development
instruction, definition of 113
instructional systems development
    (ISD) 56–8, 115, 146, 148
intellectual capital 60, 61
intellectual property 162–3
interaction *see* personal interaction
international access to technology,
    disparities in 180–81
Internet
    commercial impact of 3, 6–18
    defined 4
    effects on training 6, 9, 18–19
    emergence of 2
    market effect of 6–9
    openness of access 184
Intranet Immediate Instruction 132
intranets
    Clifford Chance case study
        97–100
    definition of term 4
    extent of usage 32, 38, 39
ISD *see* instructional systems
    development

Kay, John 28
Kirkpatrick, D. L. 165
knowledge management 62–3, 66–7
    'common knowledge' concept
        66–7
    convergence with performance
        management and training 64–5
    transfer of knowledge 67
knowledge workers 27, 30
Kolb, David 117

learndirect 183
    case study 192–6
    e-moderating job outline 153–4

learner-centred interventions 70–71,
    138, 139
learner-centred measurement 165
learner support 108–27, 149–56
    conceptual issues 113–16
    e-moderating 144, 150–52,
        153–4
    individual preferences 116–20
    key questions 126
    motivation 120–21
    one-to-one support 155
    provision of space and time
        121–4
    related to learning needs and
        platforms for delivery 109–10
    self-managed learning groups
        154, 156
    system architecture 143, 144
learners
    acceptability of e-learning to
        124–5
    importance of focusing on needs of
        42–3, 45, 108
    motivation of 120–21
    responsibility for own learning
        70
learning
    barriers to 121
    declaration on 187
    definitions of 5, 113
    distinguished from training 5,
        54–5, 113
    Honey's assertions about 117–18
    single- and double-loop 58–9
    theoretical frameworks 113–19
learning cycle 117, 118–19
learning needs see training needs
learning organisation 58–62, 67–70
    aspirational nature of 58, 68, 70
    defined 67
    focus on e-learning 69–70
    links with knowledge management
        62–3
    model of 68
learning portals 43, 46
    questionnaire to determine
        reaction to 127, 128, 130
learning resource centres 121–2, 124
    Motorola case study 133
    The Post Office case study 102
    see also places for learning
learning styles/preferences 116–19

learning systems
    costs 78
    definition of term 44
    supplier-led nature of market 44–5
    system architecture 45–6, 143–4
learning theory, definition of 113
Lewis, Nancy 124
lifelong learning 182–3
Linux 187
locations for learning see places for
    learning
'low touch' goods and services 11

m-learning/m-training 5
Management Development Associates
    (case study) 171–4
market aspects of training 81, 161–2
market clearance 81
market effect, of the Internet 6–9
Masie, Elliott 42–4, 122, 150, 163
Mayo, Andrew 67–8
McKinsey 26
MDA see Management Development
    Associates
memory see recall
mental models 59
mentoring 155
metrics for e-learning 163
Meyer, Christopher 12–13, 61, 76
moderators see e-moderating
modularisation 44
Molenda, Michael 127
Moore's Law 2
motivation to learn 120–21
Motorola 85, 122, 131–4
Mumford, Alan 117, 118

National Standards for Training
    and Development 140–41
Nonaka, Ikujiro 62

online recruitment 8–9
open-source movement 184–7
organisational learning 58–9, 60–62
organisational surround 122–4
Orton, Peter 124

paradigms
    characteristics of new training
        paradigm 70–71, 138, 139
    definition of term 53
    paradigm shifts 53–4

performance management
    convergence with training and
        knowledge management 64–5
    definition of 64
    Ernst & Young case study 72–4
personal interaction, need for 52, 85
personalisation of learning systems
    46
places for learning
    British Airways case study 135–6
    metaphorical classification of
        115–16
    survey on preferences 122, 123
    see also learning resource centres
portal sites 43
Post Office (case study) 100–104
pragmatists (learning style) 119
pre-course testing 172
price competition 7, 10
professional services delivery model
    145
promotion of learning systems 143
protocols 2, 4

questionnaires
    evaluation of web-based courses
        167–70
    on reactions to learning portals
        128–30

recall, rate of 148
recruitment methods 8–9
reflectors (learning style) 119
remembering see recall
resource-based strategy 27, 28
resource management 163–70
retailing see consumer e-commerce
robust decisions 77

s-business model (parody) 144
Sachs, J. 180–81
Salmon, Gilly 150–51
Scarbrough, Harry 62, 63
Schon, Donald 58
Schreiber, Deborah 148
scope of learning systems 143–4
self-managed learning groups
    154, 156
self-managed learning processes
    157
Senge, Peter 59–60
single frames 15, 79–84

single-loop organisational
    learning 58–9
social inclusion 179–83
soft skills training, need for interaction
    52, 85
soft technology 110, 111, 142,
    143–4
software see learning systems; open-
    source movement
Stallman, Richard 186
Stewart, Tom 61
supply chain see value chain
SWOT analysis 82, 83
synchronous learning 41, 114, 115
system architecture
    hard technology components
        45–6
    soft technology components
        143–4
systematic reflection 117
systematic training model 55–8
systems thinking 59–60

talent management 26
team learning 59
technology-based training
    definition of term 3
    emergence of 36
    Hanover Housing Association case
        study 91–6
    limitations of 85
terminology and definitions 3–5
theorists (learning style) 119
Thornburg, David 115, 116
360-degree feedback (case studies)
    72–4, 175–6
time
    as a critical resource 164–5
    learners' preferences concerning
        121–4
    timeshifting 43, 115
trainers
    ASTD study on roles and skills
        of 145–6, 147
    design and delivery skills 146,
        148–9
    expertise in soft technology
        142–4
    facilitator and deliverer roles
        distinguished 139, 141–2
    functional analysis of role of
        140–41

functional specialisms of 139,
146
roles in implementation of
e-learning 146, 147
training
characteristics of new paradigm
70–71, 138, 139
convergence with performance
management and knowledge
management 64–5
definition of term 5
developments in USA 38–44
distinguished from learning 5,
54–5, 113
effects of the Internet 6, 9, 18–19
high-tech/high-touch delivery
model 144–5
implications of connected
economy for 4, 6, 9–10, 12,
18–19, 159–60
influences and dilemmas in
training environment 27, 29
as a market 81, 161–2
opportunities presented by
technology 35–7
systematic training model 55–8
UK surveys on 31–3
value/supply chain 81–2, 161–3
training cycle *see* systematic training
model
training needs 56, 58, 109
transformation frameworks
e-business 15–18
e-learning 79–81
learning 113, 114, 115
transmission frameworks 113, 114,
115

United States
executive education network 160
instructional systems development
56–8, 146, 148
trends in use of learning
technologies 38–40
work of Elliott Masie 42–4
universities *see* corporate universities;
higher education
University for Industry 182–3
see also **learndirect**
usage analysis 46, 165
user questionnaires 128–30, 167–70

value chain
applied to training 81–2, 161–3
definition of term 11–12, 81
effect of Internet on 11–12
value web 81
Van Buren, Mark E. 38
venues for learning *see* places for
learning
virtual classrooms 41, 90, 106
virtual reality 132–3
virtual teamworking 51, 176
voice-over Internet protocol (VOIP)
41

war for talent 26
Weaver, Pete 110
web design 149
website for training community,
need for 190
World Wide Web 4
see also Internet

Xebec McGraw-Hill 32

Chartered Institute of Personnel and Development

Customer Satisfaction Survey

*We would be grateful if you could spend a few minutes answering these questions and return the postcard to CIPD. <u>Please use a black pen to answer.</u> **If you would like to receive a free CIPD pen, please include your name and address.*** IPD MEMBER Y/N

....

1. Title of book ....

2. Date of purchase: month .... year ....

3. How did you acquire this book?
☐ Bookshop ☐ Mail order ☐ Exhibition ☐ Gift ☐ Bought from Author

4. If ordered by mail, how long did it take to arrive:
☐ 1 week ☐ 2 weeks ☐ more than 2 weeks

5. Name of shop .... Town... Country...........

6. Please grade the following according to their influence on your purchasing decision with 1 as least influential: (please tick)

	1	2	3	4	5
Title					
Publisher					
Author					
Price					
Subject					
Cover					

7. On a scale of 1 to 5 (with 1 as poor & 5 as excellent) please give your impressions of the book in terms of: (please tick)

	1	2	3	4	5
Cover design					
Paper/print quality					
Good value for money					
General level of service					

8. Did you find the book:
Covers the subject in sufficient depth ☐ Yes ☐ No
Useful for your work ☐ Yes ☐ No

9. Are you using this book to help:
☐ In your work ☐ Personal study ☐ Both ☐ Other (please state)

Please complete if you are using this as part of a course

10. Name of academic institution...

11. Name of course you are following? ....

12. Did you find this book relevant to the syllabus? ☐ Yes ☐ No ☐ Don't know

Thank you!

To receive regular information about CIPD books and resources call 020 8263 3387.

1795/05/00

BUSINESS REPLY SERVICE
Licence No WD 1019

Publishing Department

Chartered Institute of Personnel and Development

CIPD House

Camp Road

Wimbledon

London

SW19 4BR